P9-DMO-576

Michael James is the author of *The Quiltmaker's Handbook*, published by Prentice-Hall. He has written numerous articles for *Quilter's Newsletter Magazine* and has lectured and conducted workshops on quilt design throughout the United States and abroad. Mr. James is recipient of a 1978 Craftsmen's Fellowship from the National Endowment for the Arts and a 1979 Craftsmen's Fellowship from the Artists' Foundation of Boston. His work has been exhibited internationally and is included in numerous corporate and private collections.

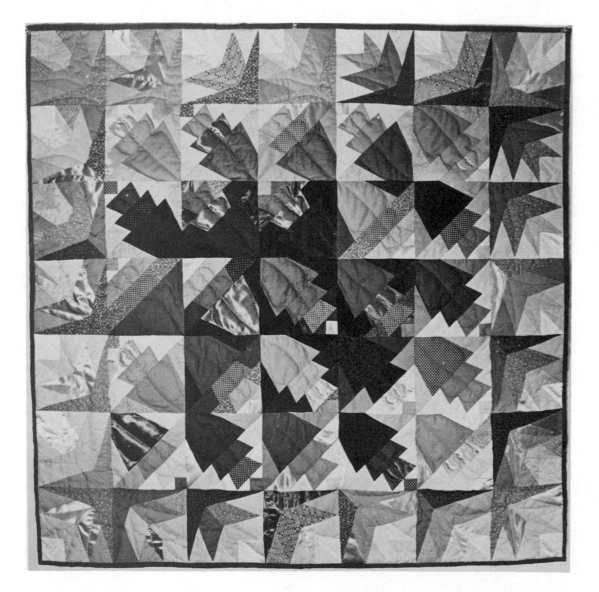

MICHAEL JAMES

The Second Quiltmaker's Handbook

Creative Approaches to Contemporary Quilt Design

A SPECTRUM BOOK

PRENTICE-HALL, INC., Englewood Cliffs, New Jersey 07632

Library of Congress Cataloging in Publication Data

James, Michael, 1949-
    The second quiltmaker's handbook.

    (Creative handcrafts series)   (A Spectrum Book)
    Bibliography: p.
    Includes index.
    1. Quilting.   I. Title.
TT835.J35   746.9'7   80-22451
ISBN   0-13-797795-6
ISBN   0-13-797787-5 (pbk.)

To my parents

Cover: *Quintet* by the author. Copyright 1980. 68 in. by 68 in.
(173 cm by 173 cm). Machine-pieced and hand-quilted cotton;
polyester batting. Collection of Mr. and Mrs. Jim Wallace. *Quintet* is a
strip-pieced quilt that employs eight sets of six colors,
each set made up into two reversed size groupings. This quilt was inspired
by the drawing shown in Fig. 5-11 on page 97. It suggests
the potential for creating strong surface movement and spatial illusions
that lies within combinations of strip piecing and curved seams.

Frontispiece: *Winter Cactus* by the author. Copyright 1978. 42 in. by 42 in.
(107 cm by 107 cm). Machine-pieced, hand-quilted cotton, satin, and velveteen;
polyester batting. Collection of Mr. and Mrs. John Middleton.

Editorial/production supervision by Louise M. Marcewicz
Insert designed by Christine Gehring Wolf
Manufacturing buyer: Cathie Lenard

Printed in the United States of America

10   9   8   7   6

Prentice-Hall International, Inc., *London*
Prentice-Hall of Australia Pty. Limited, *Sydney*
Prentice-Hall of Canada, Ltd., *Toronto*
Prentice-Hall of India Private Limited, *New Delhi*
Prentice-Hall of Japan, Inc., *Tokyo*
Prentice-Hall of Southeast Asia Pte. Ltd., *Singapore*
Whitehall Books Limited, *Wellington, New Zealand*

Contents

Preface   vii

1   INTRODUCTION   1

THE ALL-AMERICAN ART, 1
THE CONUNDRUM: WHAT IS ART? 2
SO, WHAT ABOUT QUILT ART? 4
DESIGN AND THE NEW QUILT SURFACE, 5
A PERSONAL NOTE, 5

2   FABRIC GEOMETRY: DESIGNING THE PIECED QUILT   7

SYMMETRICAL DESIGN, 7
ASYMMETRICAL DESIGN, 12
SYMMETRY VERSUS ASYMMETRY, 16
DESIGNING ASYMMETRICAL PATTERNS, 17
A SELECTION OF ASYMMETRICAL STUDIES, 27

3   COLOR DESIGN FOR THE PIECED QUILT   34

ABOUT MATERIALS FOR THE COLOR EXERCISES, 34
LIGHT AND DARK CONTRAST, 35
PURE COLOR, 36
VALUE, 39

COMPLEMENTARY COLORS, 45
ADJACENT COLORS, 46
COLOR TEMPERATURE, 47
THE EXPRESSIVE FACTOR, 51
A SPECTRUM OF CONTEMPORARY QUILTS, 52

4 THE CURVED SEAM: DESIGN AND CONSTRUCTION 54

LINEAR PATTERNS, 56
AN EXERCISE IN SPONTANEOUS COLOR SELECTION, 62
THE CRAFT OF THE CURVED SEAM, 65
A GALLERY OF CURVED-SEAM QUILTS, 82

5 STRIP PIECING THE QUILT SURFACE 87

THE TECHNIQUE OF STRIP PIECING, 87
DESIGN FOR STRIP PIECING, 95
THE CONTEMPORARY STRIP QUILT, 100

6 LOG CABIN: NEW WAYS WITH AN OLD FORM 106

THE LOG CABIN STRUCTURE, 107
COLOR DISCOVERIES WITH LOG CABIN, 118
CONTEMPORARY LOG CABIN TECHNIQUES, 121
CONTEMPORARY LOG CABIN QUILTS, 129

7 QUILTING: LINE AND TEXTURE
IN THE QUILT SURFACE 136

THE WHOLE-CLOTH QUILT 137
NOTES ON QUILTING DESIGN FOR PIECED WORK
    AND APPLIQUÉ, 146
NEW EXPLORATIONS IN WHOLE-CLOTH, 151

APPENDIXES

APPENDIX A: THE FLOWERING OF PIECED QUILT DESIGN, 161
APPENDIX B: NOTES ON FABRIC FOR QUILTS AND ITS CARE, 164
APPENDIX C: NOTES ON TAKING YOUR QUILT'S PICTURE, 167

Bibliography 178

Index 181

Preface

When I wrote *The Quiltmaker's Handbook*, interest in the history and technique of traditional American quiltmaking was higher than it had ever been. As a definitive manual on the technical processes of making quilts, the book reflected that widespread interest. Through reproductions of innovative work by contemporary American quiltmakers it also afforded the reader a look at how the tradition has continued to inspire new directions in quilt surface design.

I am pleased to know that interest in the art of the quilt continues to grow. As quiltmakers master technical processes, discover new ones, encounter new materials, and recognize the nonfunctional as well as the functional nature of the quilt, they begin to look beyond the traditional pattern. Quilts can be expressive of more than hearth and home and Americana, and quiltmakers are discovering that.

This book comes in response to the desire shared by many contemporary quiltmakers who want to express a more personal viewpoint or an inner vision through their quilts. Based on material I have worked with extensively in quilt design workshops throughout the United States and Canada, *The Second Quiltmaker's Handbook* is planned to suggest creative approaches to the design of the quilt surface.

It contains detailed discussions of the various elements of two-dimensional design as these relate to quilts, including a comprehensive chapter on color for the quiltmaker. Time-saving sewing techniques not presented in *The Quiltmaker's Handbook* are demonstrated here, and introductory treatment of the Log Cabin and strip-piecing techniques in the first book are now expanded to demonstrate their creative potential.

This book is intended primarily as a workbook, and contains two-dimensional design exercises that I feel are of particular benefit to the quiltmaker attempting to make that departure from traditional patterns. These exercises will also interest quiltmaking instructors, who I hope will be inspired by them to develop ideas to suit the needs of their own students. In the quilts represented and discussed, practicing quilt artists will find inspiration and encouragement to pursue their own images. Finally, stitchers in areas such as embroidery and needlepoint, who share many of the same design concerns as quiltmakers, will find much of the content of this book relevant to their own needs.

I hope the reader will consider this book a starting point. I hope it will lead to exciting investigations, individual attitudes and opinions, and new images.

Thanks to each of the artists who gave me permission to photograph and reproduce their work in these pages, and thanks as well to each artist who sent photographs of her work.

My students have been wonderful teachers. I thank them for taking me along on their investigations and explorations.

My wife Judy reminds me that she deserves a medal for putting up with my total preoccupation with this project. She's right of course. Thank you, Judy.

All photographs and illustrations are by the author unless otherwise indicated.

Michael James
Somerset Village, Massachusetts

viii

1 Introduction

THE ALL-AMERICAN ART

When a stranger asks me what I do, and I reply that I make quilts and teach and write about contemporary quiltmaking, he or she inevitably offers that a mother, grandmother, or wife made or makes quilts, and that some of those are in the family and are treasured heirlooms. These encounters take place not only at quilt shows or demonstrations, where I would expect to meet people interested in quilts, but also in airport lounges and aboard jetliners, in taxis, at dinner parties, in theaters, and on jogging trails.

My first feelings of surprise at this widespread identification with a historical folk art form have changed to curiosity. Now I wish I had statistics that would tell me just how many people have had a conscious or subconscious encounter with the visual arts through a quilt or related patchwork surface. How many young children have awakened to the physical warmth of the textile sandwich and the visual warmth of colors and shapes contrasting on its surface? How many people have at one time or another put together pieces of fabric with the idea of making a patchwork design, or have thought of doing so?

In the United States, where the art of geometric pieced work and the art of symmetrical appliqué were formalized in the nineteenth century, quiltmaking was and remains one of the most popular visual arts. Whether it is decorative art or folk art or fine art is another question. What is significant is that appreciation of the quilt and involvement in quiltmaking were and are spread through all corners of society.

Women developed the art of quiltmaking, and today most quilt-makers are still women. Beyond that, it's difficult to describe the average quiltmaker. She can be young or old, rich, poor, or anywhere in between. She may have learned her craft at her mother's knee, or at the local community college. She may never have completed grade school, or she may hold an advanced degree. She may live in a penthouse apartment, or in a wood-heated farmhouse. She may make quilts to keep warm, or to leave as a legacy, or to evoke a traditional past. On the other hand, she may make quilts to explore design ideas and thus build on or depart from that tradition.

Some men have also been quiltmakers, though historically their numbers have been small. In certain countries, Turkey and Syria among them, men working as artisans in small shops make quilts for the local market. For the most part, however, those men who make quilts do so for the same reasons that motivate women. Today more men are learning the craft, and even larger numbers are becoming interested (if unwitting) observers of the quiltmaking activities of the women they live with.

This democratic interest in quilts and quiltmaking has spread from the world of the home and family to the world of business. Dozens of magazines specializing in quilts and related needlework appear regularly. A small library of books on all aspects of quiltmaking has been published over the last decade. The quilt has become hot property for antique dealers, interior designers, and private collectors. Quilts are now found in museum and corporate collections, where the best examples are recognized as much more than the work of "nervous ladies."

With such widespread interest and involvement have come questions from both insiders and outsiders about the nature of quiltmaking as art, both past and present.

THE CONUNDRUM: WHAT IS ART?

While I was a student in art school I often found myself involved in discussions on that question. There were always as many opinions as there were people to offer them.

Some felt that art is the expression of beautiful things, feelings, or ideas. Others felt that art *is* beautiful things, feelings, or ideas. Some pessimistic souls said that art is the by-product of our refusal to acknowledge the hopelessness of the human condition, while some others felt that art comes of our attempts to deal with that hopeless condition. I don't remember what I thought.

Now I feel that art is what results when a person attempts to make something that he or she feels is beautiful and that, when completed, bears the unique fingerprint of the mind and hand that created it. Some would qualify that further by saying that the expression, whatever its form, must be recognized as beautiful by the general society, or by its specific audience. I don't think that's necessary. With an audience comes the interference of social mores, fashion, politics, and personal taste. To be art, an art activity and its art product need simply be.

Some works of art are the products of artistic intent. The artist consciously or subconsciously wrestles with art or design problems. Sometimes he or she deals with these for their own sake, and sometimes with the desire to resolve a larger whole. Usually, but not always, this artist has some formal art training and sometimes, but not always, what he or she does is called fine art.

The terms naive art or folk art imply an absence of formal art training and a lack of aesthetic sophistication. They also suggest honesty of expression and freedom from pretense and affectation. Very often these expressions are rooted in the lives and experiences of culturally isolated people.

Decorative art deliberately seeks to make an environment more attractive. While it can also be fine art or folk art, it has a function to adorn.

Some people feel that art is made only by artists, and when so defined it's easy to identify. I think these people imply that the artist has art training and speaks in terms that only artists understand. The trouble I have with this view is that I see around me people who intend to create art but only talk themselves and others into believing they do. I also see people who study art subjects and use the vocabulary and the accoutrements but who never produce anything to suggest that they have even one original artistic idea.

I think that the creation of great art is a rare phenomenon. It is something that may begin with an artist's idea, but is built as much on the passage of time and the steady yet evolving appeal of the work. It transcends its medium and its craft to express something that can be universally felt and appreciated.

Short of that kind of infrequent greatness is a large body of work produced by artists in a long list of disciplines. Each discipline includes work that is fine art, but also work that embodies folk, primitive, naive, or decorative art. What they all share is the process of seeking after beauty, out of which they materialized. That search for beauty may be subconscious, shadowed by other concerns. It may on the other hand be conscious. The artist may acknowledge it, or may just as likely deny it. Ultimately, the evidence is in the work itself.

SO, WHAT ABOUT QUILT ART?

Before the Industrial Revolution began to alter societies, quilts were made primarily because they were needed to keep bodies warm. No one thought to hang a quilt on a wall and thereby relieve it of that function. If the quiltmaker had time and materials and patterns to copy or an imaginative mind, she might decorate the surface of the quilt. Then it might provide emotional as well as physical warmth. But that had little to do with the reason for making quilts.

During the eighteenth and nineteenth centuries this began to change. The production of material goods cheaply and on a vast scale affected the quiltmaker's outlook on her work. Even if she couldn't afford to buy commercially manufactured bedding, the awareness that it was available would force her to acknowledge reasons for making quilts other than physical or economic necessity. Quiltmaking now became primarily a decorative art.

Certainly there are historical and contemporary quilt surfaces that go beyond decoration. What each of those shares is the clear imprint of originality that rescues it from mere prettiness and mediocrity.

Not all quilts have this imprint. The larger number are lifeless and anonymous copies of familiar patterns. They represent an art form, but do not embody art. Others, both old and new, are failed conscious or subconscious attempts to make something beautiful and original or personal. They may represent an intellectual or emotional art process that didn't fulfill the intent.

Those quilts that do succeed as folk, naive, decorative, or fine art do so because the quiltmaker had an idea and found the means to express it. That means involved either an intuitive or a learned application of design principles. In fewer cases the quiltmaker also gave a special personality and spirit to the image. Though I can't often divine its source, I sense that it's there.

DESIGN AND THE NEW QUILT SURFACE

Whether you feel that the activity of sewing pieces of colored fabrics together to make a design is folk, decorative, or fine art, you will admit that it is unnecessary. If all you want is a quilt, then three layers of textile material laid one over the other will do the trick. That sandwich, after all, is the quilt.

The object that traditionally functioned as bedcover is for all practical purposes obsolete. It serves as art form because there is a unique quality about a stitched-fabric surface design that can be duplicated in no other medium. It survives also because it can be art, enriching our daily experience of ourselves and our world.

I think that the economic and functional obsolescence of the quilt imposes a critical demand on contemporary quiltmakers. The surface design must be the best that can be realized. That design must also be inextricable from the nature of the textile sandwich itself and the materials used. The design of a surface must have something to do with its being a part of a quilt. If not, the object itself must then change and become something else. By surface design I mean the composition of the image on the top of the quilt. It is the wholeness that comes with the interplay of shapes, lines, colors, fabrics, textures, and stitches with the art idea.

Traditional quiltmakers have prided themselves on the fact that they didn't knowingly speak an art or design language. This kind of reverse elitism developed out of a fear that if the work became conscious art activity, the traditional heritage would be tainted or even lost. Art and design, as inseparable as they are from daily human life, were still misunderstood as the preoccupation of a select few.

In the quilt world that reluctance to acknowledge the design and making of quilts as potential ends in themselves dissolved in the 1970s. Some quiltmakers began to look at the design of the quilt surface with serious and deliberate artistic intent. For them it became more than a hobby or pastime or diversion. Their intent emphasized that quilt art had a future as well as a past.

A PERSONAL NOTE

When I begin to design a quilt, I want to make something beautiful. Beyond that, I make no other demands. I can't afford to. If I do, the design will fight me all the way. I begin to juxtapose fabric, and then

5

watch and read colors and shapes and textures in different combinations. I keep what strikes me, but not insistently. I must be flexible and must defer to the image when it wants to go its own way. Since I make quilts simply for the sake of doing them and answer to no external restrictions or specifications, I am privileged to be able to follow wherever that dialogue with the surface leads.

If I am very lucky, the final result will please me and others. But I won't be content with that. I'll be satisfied only if I feel that the work says something new about my involvement with the interaction of design, materials, and technique. It will succeed for me only if it says that I am here, now, and looking ahead.

I don't happen to think that anything will be lost by experimenting with new images. I think more will be lost if we don't. This is the reason for this book.

Fabric Geometry: Designing The Pieced Quilt

2

SYMMETRICAL DESIGN

If you asked almost any quiltmaker to describe some general characteristics of pieced quilt patterns, the answer would likely include references to symmetry, to repeat block structures, and to geometric shapes. Most traditional quilt patterns are symmetrical arrangements of squares, triangles, rhomboids, and other shapes, and become intriguing overall surfaces when, as block repeats, they are arranged one against another numerous times.

These symmetrical geometric block patterns became the mainstay of pieced quilt design because of their basic simplicity and the ease with which new patterns and/or variations could be created. By manipulating as few as three proportional template shapes, such as a 2-in. (5-cm) square, a 2-in. (5-cm) right triangle, and a 4-in. (10-cm) right triangle, a quiltmaker could invent hundreds of different block patterns. Many of these same patterns could likewise be created by folding paper into geometric configurations, or by drafting the designs directly with ruler and pencil, sometimes on grid sheets. However the quilt maker chose to create block patterns, the end result was almost always a symmetrical design.

WHAT IS SYMMETRY?

Symmetry is defined as "the correspondence, in size, form, and arrangement, of parts on opposite sides of a plane, line, or point." (*The American College Dictionary*. New York: Random House, Inc. 1966.) In most traditional quilt block patterns, this symmetry is either bilateral or quadrilateral. Bilateral symmetry involves the equal arrangement of shapes on either side of one axis. This axis may be real, as defined by a seam line, or imaginary. It may move across the block between two opposite sides or two opposite corners, dividing the pattern into halves, as in Fig. 2-1.

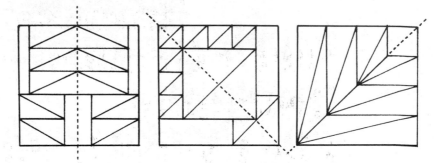

Figure 2-1. Block designs displaying bilateral symmetry.

Quadrilateral symmetry exists when the shapes in the design are arranged equally on opposite sides of two real or imaginary axes whose intersection at the center of the design creates 90-degree angles. The side-to-side or corner-to-corner crossing of these axes thus creates a block pattern that divides into quarters, as in Fig. 2-2.

Figure 2-2. Block designs displaying quadrilateral symmetry.

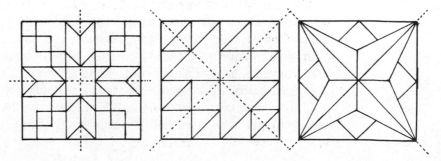

Some traditional pieced block patterns, such as Mariner's Compass and Dresden Plate, display radial symmetry. Shapes are repeated on opposite sides of a central point, and the seam lines become the radiating axes. These patterns usually convey a sense of energy generated out from the central point (see Fig. 2-3).

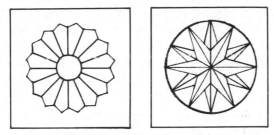

Figure 2-3. Block designs displaying radial symmetry.

In addition to symmetrical arrangement of shapes, the traditional repeat block depends as well on symmetrical distribution of color and on light and dark contrasts. The relative weight that each shape has, depending on its color and whether it is a dark or light value, is equalized by its corresponding shape on the opposite side of the axis (or axes). The balance that results is usually obvious; the visual impression made by shapes repeated equally on the sides of axes tells the viewer how this balance is achieved (see Fig. 2-4).

By itself, the symmetrical block usually reads as a static design. Its formal, rigid character, imposed by the axial arrangement, reduces

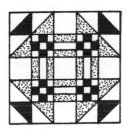

Figure 2-4. Symmetrical distributions of color and light and dark contrasts.

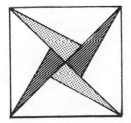

Figure 2-5. Block designs with corner-to-corner axes.

any sense of movement or activity within the boundaries of the block. Exceptions are some patterns with corner-to-corner axes. These can suggest a sense of movement or energy generated out from or in toward the center of the design (see Fig. 2-5).

We perceive a symmetrical block design as whole and complete even before it is set in multiple to form the overall quilt surface. We read the image objectively; it must "look" right.

The order that is an inherent part of the block as a unit is transferred to the overall surface when that block is multiplied. Whether the symmetrical block is repeated row by row uniformly, quarter-turned alternately, or placed against itself as a mirror image, the sense of order and balance will be maintained (see Fig. 2-6).

The multiple surface arrangement, however, will introduce spatial illusions, surface rhythm, and movement that will help to provide the dynamism usually lacking in the individual block pattern.

Nancy Halpern's *Flying Carpet* (Plate 4 and Figs. 2-7 and 2-8) is an exciting example of symmetrical design that achieves that dynamism.

Figure 2-6. *Symmetrical block pattern in multiple arrangements.* The block is set side by side without turning, then quarter-turned alternately, and finally set against itself in mirror image.

Figure 2-7. *Flying Carpet* by Nancy Halpern. 1979. 72 in. by 85 in. (183 cm by 216 cm). Machine-pieced, hand-quilted cotton and cotton blends; Dacron batting.

Figure 2-8. Detail, *Flying Carpet* by Nancy Halpern.

The primary block design is subordinated to the secondary circular patterns that are created as the blocks join. The spatial illusion created in the center of the surface by the contrast of warm reds and rusts with cool blues and greens is extended almost literally in the outside border by the use of unevenly dyed fabric that suggests a cloudy sky. Small pinwheels within each block enclose square windows, through which that blue sky reappears at the center of the quilt.

ASYMMETRICAL DESIGN

Asymmetry is the absence of symmetry. In the asymmetrical block there is no axial distribution of shape, light and dark contrasts, or color. The individual block pattern cannot be divided into identical halves, quarters, or other fractional parts. Shapes within the block seem to be arranged accidentally, or randomly.

Balance in the asymmetrical block pattern is achieved primarily through contrasts of large and small shapes, light and dark values, and bright and pale colors. Whereas symmetrical patterns create balance by matching shapes and colors on one side of an axis with those on the other, asymmetrical patterns must achieve balance by creating a tension that unifies each of the elements that make up the block.

Figure 2-9. Comparison of symmetrical and asymmetrical blocks. Both blocks are composed of the same shapes.

That tension can occur when a grouping of several small shapes is contrasted with a single larger shape. It can occur when the weight of a darker color is offset by the openness of lighter-colored areas. It can also occur when diagonal thrusts within the block are opposed by horizontal or vertical movements or both (see Fig. 2-9). Most often asymmetrical balance is achieved when each of these contrasts is employed simultaneously.

As a result, the individual asymmetrical repeat image is usually quite active, in contrast to the symmetrical pattern, which is ordinarily static. There must be an inherent sense of rhythm and movement within the asymmetrical block. The eye should move around the entire design continually, taking in its parts and reading and evaluating the contrasts around which the design is organized. However, this sense of movement, occurring within the block and demanding our participation, should not depend on directional symbols. Triangles

Figure 2-10. Directional symbols do not necessarily give a sense of movement to the asymmetrical block designs.

arranged to form arrows, for instance, lead the eye too literally and thus destroy the abstract beauty and the nonrepresentational nature of the asymmetrical block pattern (see Fig. 2-10).

THE REPEAT BLOCK SURFACE

The sense of movement and activity contained within the block is magnified when the block is arranged in multiple. Set side by side against itself without turning, the asymmetrical block becomes a surface design that achieves much of the rigidity and formality of the symmetrical design. Rotating the block by quarter turns within the set can create a secondary surface pattern that is, in effect, a symmetrical design. This also occurs when setting the blocks against themselves as mirror images. Each of these set arrangements is illustrated in Fig. 2-11, and in Fig. 2-12 the second repeat variation is multiplied to create an overall surface design.

The asymmetrical characteristics of the individual block can also be transferred to the overall quilt surface design when the blocks are set together in a random arrangement. No specific order is given to the block-to-block placement. The blocks are twisted and turned irregularly, which allows accidental connections and subpatterns to be created. The symmetrical appearance of the quarter-turn arrangement in Fig. 2-13 contrasts sharply with the effect of the random arrangement in Fig. 2-14.

Figure 2-11. Multiple arrangements of an asymmetrical design. The block in the upper left is set against itself to create five strikingly different repeat patterns.

Figure 2-12. The second repeat variation in Fig. 2-11 is multiplied here to create an overall surface design. Four large pinwheel forms become dark figures twisting in a fractured space of lighter geometric shapes.

14

Figure 2-13. An asymmetrical block shown in quarter-turn multiple arrangement.

Figure 2-14. The block design shown in Fig. 2-13 is arranged here at random. The abstract geometric pattern is built on irregular twists and turns and unexpected connections.

The contrasts that governed the creation of the single block pattern come into play once again, but on an expanded scale. The balance and rhythm achieved in the block must be extended across the entire surface of the design, and the tension that held together the elements of the block pattern must likewise unify the entire repeat surface. (See Virginia Anderson's quilt *Whirligig* in Plate 2.)

The asymmetrical block is not likely to appear as whole and complete as the symmetrical design. It depends for interest on being arranged in multiple. We perceive the single block image as well as the multiple image subjectively; it must "feel" right. A precise correspondence must be set up between color and shape, between primary and secondary images in the overall surface, and between the logical nature of the repeat grid structure and the illogical character of the single asymmetrical block composition.

SYMMETRY VERSUS ASYMMETRY

In exploring the nature of symmetrical and asymmetrical designs, we can see that the symmetrical pattern, governed by logical juxtapositions of design elements, is easier to understand. Not only is the single block divided into equal parts by axes, but so is the overall quilt surface. The formality and stability displayed in the block pattern are transferred to the primary repeat pattern and are in turn displayed in whatever subordinate surface patterns are created. These secondary patterns, often unpredictable, add interest and complexity to the surface. In addition, they can enliven the surface with additional contrasts and movements that do not occur in the single block.

The asymmetrical pattern depends on a number of less easily defined contrasts and interchanges. Shapes and their sizes, colors, and values must be arranged and rearranged until a balance of these parts is achieved. For a given set of shapes, this balance may occur in a number of different arrangements. In whatever way we arrange the shapes, they must be held together in sufficient tension to create a block design in which no one element overpowers the rest. The eye must move smoothly around the design without becoming fixed on any one shape, contrast, or other detail. This holds true for the overall surface design created from the multiplication of the single asymmetrical block in a grid structure. Any sense of movement and activity contained in the single block will be amplified in the repeat block surface. Unpredictable secondary patterns will emerge and these, along with the symmetrical grid structure, will help to organize the random geometric block pattern.

The key differences between symmetrical and asymmetrical block patterns can be summarized as follows:

Symmetrical	*Asymmetrical*
— Shapes, colors, light and dark contrasts, and other features are distributed equally by an axis or axes.	— Here there is no axial distribution. Shapes and other features are arranged at random.
— Balance is achieved by equalizing color and shape weights on either side of an axis or axes.	— Balance is achieved by contrasts and the resulting tensions that hold the shapes together.
— The single block pattern is usually static. A sense of movement occurs when the block is set against itself many times.	— The single block pattern must have an inherent sense of movement (not based on directional symbols).
— The eye takes in the individual block pattern as a whole, logical image.	— The eye must move around the design continually, reading it to make sense of it.
— The mind orders the image objectively; it must look right.	— The mind orders the image subjectively; it must feel right.
— Symmetrical patterns depend on regular repetition.	— Asymmetrical patterns depend on irregularities, twists and turns, and accidental juxtapositions.

DESIGNING ASYMMETRICAL PATTERNS

The process of creating an original block design and, in turn, an original repeat block surface should involve a series of open-minded encounters with shapes in different sizes, colors, and values. Any creative exploration should anticipate and take advantage of the unexpected—quiltmaking no less than dance, painting, or pottery. To set in motion a series of contrasts and harmonies and then to organize and refine them, searching for the tensions that breathe life into the image, is the essence of designing.

How we design is a highly individual matter. Many quiltmakers are comfortable working with the basic grid in the form of graph paper, marking shapes on the grid with pencil and ruler, and later applying color to the design. Some quiltmakers enjoy folding paper squares to invent a design, later reproducing the folded pattern as a line drawing on paper. Others feel more confident going right to fabric, cutting and sewing spontaneously, and allowing the surface design to develop along the way. No one method is preferable to the others, and no one is guaranteed to produce successful results at every work session.

I developed the system described below for exploring asymmetrical block and surface patterns after having employed a number of different approaches in planning some of my own quilts, as well as in conducting workshops in quilt design. Short of cutting directly into fabric, this process allows a great amount of spontaneity to enter into the work. It cannot be relied on to do the designing; the eye and mind of the quiltmaker must orchestrate the juxtapositions. As an exercise device, however, it is simple and direct, and can be used effectively by the beginner as well as by the advanced quilt designer. It is also applicable to designing symmetrical images.

This cut-paper method will be approached in two parts. In this chapter, we will work in black and white and two intermediate gray values. We will concentrate on resolving designs based on shape variations, light and dark contrasts, and movement. In Chapter 3, I will suggest ways in which color may be applied to the design through the use of the cut-paper process.

MATERIALS

The items necessary for working with this method, if not already on hand, can be found in any well-stocked art supply shop. Common sense will indicate when substitutions can be made without affecting the end result.

You will need one 9-in. by 12-in. (23-cm by 30.5-cm) sheet each of white, light gray, dark gray, and black construction paper. I recommend construction paper because it is widely available and inexpensive. Artist's charcoal paper in these tones may be substituted, and silkscreen-coated Color-Aid-type papers may also be used. Do not substitute a color for any of the neutral tones in this set. Be careful as well that the grays you select are in fact neutral. A green-gray or a blue-gray, for instance, will change the impartial character of the images. The intent here is to deal purely with the linear and tonal composition of the block. Color introduces an entire range of additional problems and associations that will be dealt with separately.

You will need either a pair of paper-cutting scissors, a paper cutter, or a razor-bladed knife to cut these sheets.

You will also need four artist's colored pencils: one each of white, light gray, dark gray, and black. These should approximate each of the neutral values in paper. The colored pencils should have an oil base rather than a chalk base. Pastel pencils are unsuitable. You may duplicate the two grays, if necessary, by creating these tones with mixtures of the white and black pencils, but this will require additional time. In the absence of white pencil you may leave white areas in the design uncolored, and you may use a regular No. 2 pencil applied with varying pressures to duplicate the grays and the black. In whatever way you create the four neutrals, each should be clear and distinct from the others.

Have a pencil sharpener handy to keep these pencils well pointed. You will also need a ruler.

As you create block designs, you will copy them on a basic grid sheet or graph paper. This graph may be made up of five squares, four squares, or two squares to the linear inch (or per 2.5 cm).

You will use several sheets of extra-heavyweight tracing paper for rendering the single block patterns in multiple. This should be the heaviest tracing stock available: a 110-weight paper will work well. The colored pencil impressions to be made on this paper should be opaque, and so the paper should be durable.

DESIGNING A BLOCK PATTERN

First, you will need to prepare the set of paper shapes with which you will work out the designs. On the white sheet, rule and draw the diagram shown in Fig. 2-15. Start by dividing the page into twelve 3-in. (7.5-cm) squares, then subdivide these as indicated.

Next put the four construction paper sheets together, with the white diagram on top. Cut through all sheets simultaneously, on each line in the diagram, as in Fig. 2-16. You will now have an assortment of 152 pieces.

The design process begins as soon as you choose any one shape and place it before you. Keeping in mind the characteristics of asymmetrical patterns discussed above, begin placing shapes one against another. Be aware of light and dark contrasts as they occur, and watch how they give linear definition to the design. Remember that since there is no axial balance in an asymmetrical design, you will have to be especially aware of how contrasts of small and large shapes are employed to create balance. In addition, you will want to watch diagonal oppositions to horizontal and vertical movements in the design, as these can also be used effectively to achieve balance.

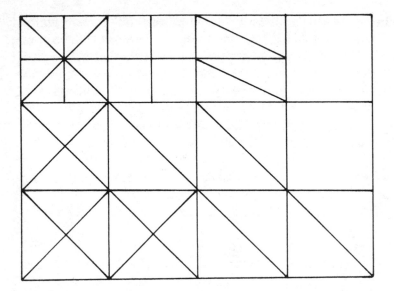

Figure 2-15. Diagram for drafting cut-paper shapes.

Figure 2-16. The four construction-paper sheets are held together and cut simultaneously.

In your first explorations, you may wish to work out designs that fit into the traditional structures, such as three-patch (or nine-patch), four-patch, or five-patch. This orientation will provide a concrete framework within which you can build the abstract image.

20

Don't belabor an image that isn't coming together. As you juxtapose different shapes and values, contrasts and tensions will develop that will give direction and momentum to your work. When this doesn't seem to be happening, start again. Approaching the design problem with a preconceived idea of what the image should look like when complete will set obstacles in your path. Let the cut-paper shapes make suggestions, and then respond to them.

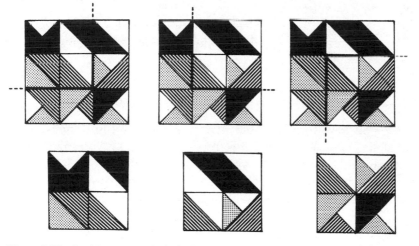

Figure 2-17. In this asymmetrical block smaller groupings of shapes can be isolated to become independent repeat block designs.

Figure 2-18. Cut-paper block design is drafted onto grid sheet.

You may find on occasion that a block that doesn't seem to be working right contains within itself one or two or more smaller groupings of shapes that can be removed from the larger design to become independent repeat images (Fig. 2-17). Study each pattern you develop for just such secondary designs. Isolate them for subsequent reproduction as multiple repeat images.

Once you have completed a block pattern in cut paper, duplicate the image as closely as possible in colored pencil directly on graph paper, as in Fig. 2-18.

This copy should be a small sketch, approximately 1½ in. (3.8 cm) square. Be careful that the shapes and tones in the sketch match the cut-paper model.

CREATING A REPEAT SURFACE DESIGN

After you have drafted a half dozen or so different blocks on the graph sheet, choose one that interests you most. You will render this one in multiple to see what overall surface patterns can be created. Lay the tracing paper sheet over the original drawing of the block and trace the drawing in the neutral tones, as shown in Fig. 2-19.

Figure 2-19. Block is copied onto heavyweight tracing paper in a uniform side-by-side arrangement.

Figure 2-20. Colored pencil tracing of the asymmetrical block set against itself sixteen times, four by four.

Bear down heavily with the colored pencil, so that your block images are bold and opaque. Faint, feather-light impressions convey the feeling that you're not very sure of what you're doing; bear down with the pencil confidently, even though at first that self-confidence may be tentative.

You will probably need to reproduce your block image against itself at least nine times (three by three) and possibly up to sixteen times (four by four) in order to get a full picture of the surface design possibilities (see Fig. 2-20).

You will find it helpful, after tracing the block in multiple, to cut the blocks apart. This will allow you to twist and turn them against each other, or to flip them over to create mirror images (see Fig. 2-21). Once you have resolved an arrangement that satisfies you, glue it down permanently.

You can use manipulation of cut-paper shapes to create abstract geometric surface arrangements that are independent of the block repeat structure (Fig. 2-22). The principles of asymmetrical balance discussed above also apply in the nonrepeat composition. The absence of a modular repeat structure, however, makes resolution of the final arrangement more difficult to achieve.

Figure 2-21. Tracing is cut apart and rearranged to form various patterns.

Figure 2-22. An asymmetrical geometric composition that does not depend on the repeat block structure.

Traditional quilts almost inevitably had borders. These were attached to make the quilt larger, or to balance an elaborate pieced or appliqué design with a plain field of color, or because the quiltmaker thought that every quilt should have a border. Certain designs do seem to need a border to contain them.

After arranging your block in multiple, study the overall image to determine if a border (or borders) should become part of the design. Does the pattern seem to want to run off into space? Does it seem fractured or unstructured? A border repeat can sometimes work to organize or stabilize an otherwise busy pattern. It can provide a sense

Figure 2-23. Asymmetrical three-patch block pattern arranged in a quarter-turn repeat of nine blocks.

of rhythm to the design, and can also help the eye to move around the surface.

You can often find border elements within the block pattern itself, or in shapes that are created between blocks that are set together in multiple. Sometimes border designs are new images independent of the block repeat. Where they come from is less important than how they relate visually to the surface design. This relationship is basically a question of scale. If intended to complement the main design, the border should not overwhelm it, nor should the reverse occur. It follows that the border should not be so weak that it goes unnoticed. In experimenting with border designs, the critical question to ask yourself is: Would this design work as well without the border?

The block repeat in Fig. 2-23 is a complex and active image that seems to need to be tied down with a simple repeat border. Although the combination of shapes used in the border repeat unit does not occur in the overall pattern, the rhomboid is the dominant shape in both settings. Where the border rhomboid joins with the large outer triangle in every other block, the block pattern and border merge to create a wholly integrated design.

The quilt shown in Plate 7 employs two borders effectively. Without the narrow dark brown border just outside the block repeat area, the small outer dark brown triangles in the blocks seem disconnected and fragile (see Fig. 2-28). The rust trapezoid joined to the white triangle at the outside forms a sawtooth variation which, in its regularity, acts as a relief from the intense activity at the center.

ON YOUR OWN

After you have worked for a while with the basic assortment of shapes presented in this first exercise, you may wish to put together your own collection. This might involve curves as well as straight lines, diamonds as well as squares and rectangles, rhomboids, and any number of different triangles. The variety of shapes is extensive, and the combinations possible are limitless (see Fig. 2-24).

Remember as you work with cut paper as described above that this device is only a tool to help ignite the creative process. It is not a foolproof technique for designing snappy images. It depends entirely on how well you, as designer, understand the interdependence of all the visual elements that go into making a vital surface. It also depends critically on what you feel the function of the geometric pattern is, and how you relate that function to your own work. Finally, it depends on how much of your own spirit and personality you can invest in the image, and in turn on how much spirit and personality of its own the image will project. You can be taught to put shapes and colors together pleasingly, even convincingly, but you cannot be taught how to give them life.

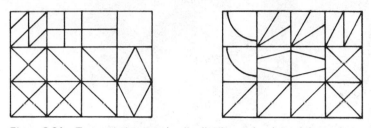

Figure 2-24. Two variations on the distribution and variety of shapes for the cut-paper exercise.

A SELECTION OF ASYMMETRICAL STUDIES

Figure 2-12 shows an asymmetrical block arranged in quarter-turn against itself sixteen times to form a symmetrical surface pattern. (Other arrangements of this block are shown in Fig. 2-11.) The single block displays a strong diagonal thrust, emphasized by the elongated white triangle that leads the diagonal seam into a corner. This arrangement of the block creates two levels of activity. The darker shapes group together to form a rotating pinwheel in each quarter of the design. These pinwheels become solid figures on the surface. In contrast, the lighter shapes group together to form an active ground on which the pinwheels twist. The touching of the pinwheels defines a lighter ground area at the center of the design, and these shapes become a larger solid form that seems to be pushing against the narrow black points.

The three-patch grid was the foundation for the block pattern repeated in Fig. 2-23. The contrast of the large black rhomboid with the white trapezoids creates the main interest in the overall design. The black figures seem to float from top to bottom and from side to side, in and out of the fractured diagonal white grid. (The border in this design is discussed above.)

Because the block design in Fig. 2-25 is divided into two rectangles, the verticality of the shape arrangement is emphasized, and as a result the surface seemed to require a rectangular format. The blocks were arranged upside down or as mirror reflections of one another or both.

Figure 2-25. The rectangular format of this asymmetrical block pattern was suggested by the two rectangular halves of the single block.

A diagonal sequence is created by the suggestion of oval shapes, and this helps to disguise the rigid rectangular structure. As shapes move quickly across the surface, the impression produced is a bit like that of a cinematic image out of synchronization.

In Fig. 2-26 a symmetrical and somewhat traditional image results from setting an unlikely asymmetrical block pattern against itself in quarter-turn. The blacks in the block join in the overall surface to define four large, tilted forms that enclose white and gray pinwheels.

Joy Van Buskirk's three-patch block (Fig. 2-27) by itself gives no indication of what will happen when it is arranged in multiple. Set against itself sixteen times in quarter-turn, it creates a pinwheel and cross image that seems to tilt slightly to the left within the square format of the overall pattern. The large, dark octagonal form that occurs in each quarter of the surface is repeated as a negative white reverse image at the center of the design. This interchange of the positive dark form and the negative white form gives this pattern a bold vitality that reflects the simplicity of the block itself.

The block repeat in Sunny Davis's *Lightning Ranger* shown in Fig. 2-28 and Plate 7 is actually a symmetrical shape arrangement rendered as an asymmetrical color composition. The block is set in quarter-turn, and as a result jagged lightning bolts seem to dart across the sur-

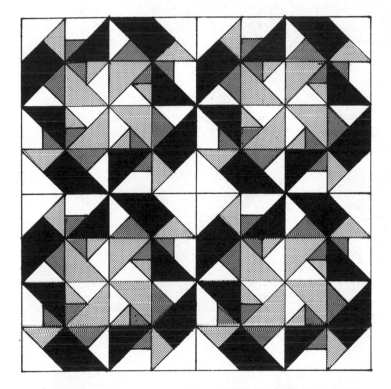

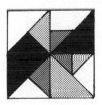

Figure 2-26. The single block in this pattern gives no idea of how the surface will organize itself when the block is arranged in multiple. Pinwheels and pinwheel variations become very visible elements of the overall surface.

Figure 2-27. Untitled pieced design by Joy Van Buskirk. Numerous secondary patterns are created in this symmetrical arrangement.

Figure 2-28. Design by Sunny Davis for a quilt entitled *Lightning Ranger.* The suggestion of transparency gives the diagonal forms an interwoven look.

face. Secondary patterns occur where the corners of blocks come together. The colors used in the quilt suggest the Southwest, and the design itself captures a feeling of native American surface decoration.

Figure 2-29 shows a block pattern in which diagonal movements are opposed by a strong horizontal and vertical structure that forms narrow rectangles along two sides of the block and a small square in the corner. The diagonals are emphasized by the dark shapes in order to keep the square and rectangular forms from overpowering

Figure 2-29. Tilted oval shapes are created in each quarter of this pattern. These help give a fluid quality to the design.

the design. Since these shapes repeat the form of the module itself, they tend to lock the eye into seeing only the square grid structure. The diagonals contradict this, and set up a secondary pattern of large oval forms. There are, of course, no curves in the design.

In *Farmscape Times Three* (Plate 6) Janie Burke has taken a large, asymmetrical geometric composition and repeated it four times. The contrast of light and dark triangles and the vertical sawtooth arrangements are the dominant organizing elements, and supporting them is a secondary network of large and small squares. The color arrangement is likewise asymmetrical, and this increases the complexity of the surface.

Virginia Anderson's *Whirligig* (Plate 2) is composed of an asymmetrical block arranged against itself randomly. Although the arrangement of shapes within the block is the same throughout the quilt, the asymmetrical color arrangement within the block is different in each repeat. The wide red velveteen border acts as a relief from the complex central composition and limits a design that could otherwise go on indefinitely.

3 Color Design For the Pieced Quilt

Part of the attraction of quiltmaking is the work with color. We experience visual and emotional satisfaction when we discover exciting color interactions. In quiltmaking the beauty of color is augmented by a wide range of types and textures in fabric, and these can give a richness to the two-dimensional design that is unique to this medium.

The best way to learn about color is to work with it. The study of color theory is invaluable but cannot replace actual physical manipulation of color within the confines of a design problem. In quiltmaking this manipulation occurs in every instance that two or more fabric colors are juxtaposed. Since most quiltmakers today are using commercially precolored yardage, awareness of how and why one color affects another is critical to developing a discriminating color sense.

ABOUT MATERIALS FOR THE COLOR EXERCISES

You can work out the color exercises in this chapter with one of several materials: colored paper, fabric, or colored pencils.

Colored paper is recommended because it can be collected from hundreds of sources and is easy to handle. You may wish to put together a collection of inexpensive construction paper by buying a number of small packages, each of a different brand. Colors vary from one paper company to another, so you'll find that the red in one package will be different from the red in another.

Screen-printed, color-coordinated papers (such as Color-Aid or Pantone) are beautiful but expensive. Their uniform matte surface and fully saturated hues make them particularly appealing.

Origami paper, also intense, makes a good complement to construction paper.

Fabric can be cut and used in place of colored paper. You may wish to cut 9 in. by 12 in. (23 cm by 30.5 cm) pieces of fabric and, with a spray adhesive, glue them to pieces of oak tag or bristol board. They can then be cut as easily as paper. The advantage to quiltmakers in experimenting with actual fabric is obvious.

A set of good-quality colored pencils can be used effectively also. These should be neither too hard nor too soft, but should produce an intense, opaque image when used on heavyweight tracing paper.

LIGHT AND DARK CONTRAST

In Chapter 2 we worked exclusively in a neutral color range to emphasize linear definition and light and dark contrast. This also helped to eliminate the personal emotional and symbolic associations we inevitably make with color. We worked with white and black and two grays. The grays chosen were neutral grays, one light and one dark. Hypothetically, each of the grays should have corresponded to two equidistant positions between white and black on a gray value scale. For the purposes of the cut-paper exercise, however, it was not critical that we be that specific.

We saw that light and dark contrast was most dramatic where white was placed against black. It was also strong when dark gray approached white and was least active when light gray and white were placed together. These contrasts helped to define the geometric composition of the block patterns we worked with in Chapter 2.

Light and dark contrast also helps to distribute weight in a two-dimensional design. The dark colors in a pattern, including black, appear heavy and solid, giving a feeling of density to those areas of the image. Lighter colors, including white, appear translucent and buoyant and seem to be filled with air. They rise to the surface of the design and may even seem to float in front of it. Dark colors, on the other hand, tend to recede from the surface, massing in the mind's eye to form a ground that anchors the lighter colors to the two-dimensional plane.

Nell Cogswell's *Aquarius Quilt* (Plate 3) demonstrates the capacity of white to work simultaneously as figure and as ground. The teepee shapes that combine to form diamonds at the center of the quilt reverse alternately between white, yellow, and blue. The four white triangles at the middle of each border, however, unify the rest of the white shapes to create the illusion of a large diamond enclosing activity in the center of the quilt. If you cover the outer white triangles, this effect is lost.

Light and dark contrast defines the geometric image of pine trees massed on a fog-shrouded island in Nancy Halpern's quilt *Fall's Island* (Plate 1). The darkest shapes are concentrated at the center of the image, suggesting the thick growth and giving a sense of depth to the surface. As we move out from the center, the block repeats become less sharply defined as the mist softens the outlines of the trees. Although a range of neutrals is used through most of the design, the image is not dull or lackluster. The dissolve from the dark mass at the center to the lighter areas suggests a fog just about to lift, saturated with a sunlight that gives richness to the colors Nancy used.

It's important to remember that all spatial effects in the two-dimensional design surface are highly variable, and depend as much on other than spatial factors such as value sequence, color temperature, and color intensity. The amount and distribution of lights and darks in a pattern also affect their activity.

In Fig. 2-12, for example, the concentration of the darkest shapes in the pinwheels causes them to contract in the surface space, pulling just behind the thick-angled cross of light shapes that appears at the center of the design. In Fig. 2-25 the dark shapes group to form a solid network through which we look at the light shapes that appear behind it. The dark shapes in Fig. 2-26 mass to become four large rotating forms on a white ground, but at the same time push four pinwheel variations out as white figures where the sides of quadrants of the design touch. This push and pull between light and dark is part of the basic nature of two-dimensional design.

PURE COLOR

The twelve colors of the standard color wheel (Plate 33) are generally regarded as pure colors. Each pure color is dense, rich, and highly saturated. It is free of any mixture with white or black.

The primaries are red, yellow, and blue; these are the sources of each of the other colors. Pure yellow is the lightest color on the wheel, both in its pure value and in its visual weight. It seems neither warm nor cool in temperature, and neither reddish nor greenish in hue. Pure red is solid and vibrant, and warm in temperature. Pure blue, on the other hand, is cool, and, in comparison with the aggressiveness of red and the liveliness of yellow, seems impartial and restrained.

The following exercise will acquaint you with various characteristics of the primary colors and will demonstrate how strongly different grounds can affect the impression made by these colors.

Choose a block design from those you recorded on graph paper in the Chapter 2 exercises. Select a block in which either the black shapes predominate or the white shapes are dominant. Each of the other three values should also be represented. You will now apply the primary colors to this block design, in two variations.

For the first block, substitute yellow, red, and blue (as pure as you can secure these in cut paper, fabric, or colored pencil) for the three subordinate tones. You will now see the primaries against either a black or white foundation.

In the second block, reverse the tone of the foundation. If in the first block you saw the primaries against black, in the second you'll see them against white. The white setting for the primary colors shows them at their highest density and opacity. They appear characteristically bold and straightforward. In a black setting they appear translucent, almost lit up from within. Here the colors seem more fragile, and a sense of mystery and additional tension enters the design (see Plate 34).

The uncomplicated correspondence between pure color and white may suggest why white foundations appear to have been most popular among traditional American quiltmakers. The colors are shown off at their boldest, and the strong contrasts help to define the design. This is also true of the relationship of white to the primary colors used in *Aquarius Quilt* in Plate 3.

Traditional Amish quiltmakers, on the other hand, reveled in juxtaposing pure colors of all sorts, and frequently set them against black backgrounds. The surfaces that resulted were often introspective and elusive.

THE SECONDARY COLORS

Halfway between the primary colors we find the secondaries. They are orange, green, and violet. Pure orange consists of an exact balance of pure yellow and pure red. Pure green consists of half yellow and half blue, neither one predominating. Similarly, pure violet is an equal admixture of primary blue and red.

Orange is the warmest color on the wheel, suggesting fire and heat. Green is cool and refreshing, and since it is midway between yellow and blue, reflects the lightness of the first and the airiness of the second. Violet is the darkest color in the spectrum. A mixture of red and blue, it displays no definite temperature but readily assumes a coolness or warmth depending on what context we place it in.

Peggy Spaeth uses the secondary colors in her quilt *Boxes and Stars* (Plate 8), activating the surface with pure orange and pure green, two additional values of each, and a single value of violet. The oranges make the strongest impression, moving solidly from side to side, while the greens seem to form suspended vertical bands anchoring the orange cubes to the quilt surface. The light violet recedes behind the floating cube forms, a cool foil for the heated exchange going on in the foreground.

The same secondary harmony is used in the Pineapple Log Cabin sampler shown in Plate 36. The contrast of the hot orange with the cool green electrifies the image. The color diffusion that begins to occur because of the jagged sawtooth created by the overlap of the fabric strips is intensified by that color contrast. The violet, which becomes background here as well, helps to anchor the color forms to the surface.

THE TERTIARY COLORS

The remaining colors on the twelve-color wheel are made of further mixtures of the primary and the secondary colors. Yellow and green provide yellow-green; green and blue give blue-green; blue and violet give blue-violet; and so on. These combinations extend the range of the primaries and secondaries and introduce more subtle and expressive harmonies and contrasts.

Turn to your own collection of quilt fabric at this point and study the range of colors represented. Select first the nearest you have to the primary colors: the yellowest yellow, the reddest red, and the bluest blue. Between these, arrange the secondary colors, or the closest approach to them you can find with your on-hand fabric. Finally, arrange any intermediate colors between these. You will want to discriminate carefully between various greens, arranging yellower greens closer to yellow, and bluer greens closer to blue, and you will want to do likewise with the balance of your fabric.

The collection of fabrics which you have on hand at any given time is your palette. Although you needn't buy by the bolt or fill every available nook and cranny of your work space with pieces of fabric, you should build a fairly broad collection of fabric color with which to do your work.

The practice of going out in search of specific colors after a project has been planned out on paper or in your imagination is inevitably frustrating — a particular color just isn't there when you need it. (You do remember seeing it six months or a year ago, but now it's out of stock or discontinued.) You're back at the drawing board, hours or perhaps days later, making changes based on what you could find, still reflecting on the quilt that might have been.

If you get in the habit of thinking of your own fabric collection, rather than the local fabric store, as your resource center, you will soon learn to keep an eye open for colors in fabric that you're weak on or that you're running short of. When you happen on a new color or colors showing subtle tonal or value modulations that set them off from colors you already own, you'll want to purchase a yard or so for your own stock. In a short time, you'll be able to recognize fabric colors that you don't already have, as well as colors that are poorly represented in your collection.

Finally, be careful that you don't limit yourself by purchasing only colors that you are actively interested in using at that particular time. You don't need to be thinking ahead, necessarily, when you buy two yards of a fabric that has particular color appeal. The fact that you do own it, however, will probably influence the creative direction you take in subtle and even subconscious ways. The same holds true for fabric colors that you don't like. Perhaps the reason you don't like them is that you've never worked with them.

VALUE

We use the word *value* to describe the degree of lightness or darkness of a color. Value is one of the most relative characteristics of color, and one of the easiest to modulate.

Every pure color is simultaneously its own pure value. If we assume that each of the twelve colors of the standard color wheel is a pure color, then we see twelve pure values as well. The pure value of a color is free of any mixture with white or black.

Every pure color can be diluted with white or black to create a full range of light or dark value. The addition of white in graduated amounts to pure color creates a scale of light values. The addition of black creates a range of dark values. The addition of white or black to a pure color does not change the color; it simply changes the value (see Fig. 3-1 and Plate 33).

What we call pink is really a light value of red. What we call lavender is really a light value of violet. Because we work in general with predetermined colors, it is important that we recognize that pink is not a different color from red, but a particular value of it. Aqua is not a different color from blue-green, but a light value of it. Brown is not a pure color, but a dark value of orange.

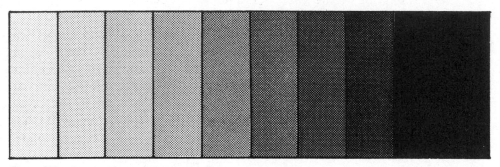

Figure 3-1. A gray value scale in ten steps.

THE VALUE SCALE

The best way to achieve a clear understanding of value is to create a series of value scales. Each scale should be rendered as a row of squares of equal size. You will need to use good-quality colored pencils, designer's gouache, or colored paper for this exercise. If you work with colored paper, you will need an extensive assortment.

Begin by choosing a pure color. Place that color in a 1-in. (2.5-cm) to 2-in. (5-cm) square on a large sheet of blank paper. Working toward white, lighten the pure color by mixing it with increasing amounts of white or by choosing a slightly lighter piece of paper. If you are working with pencil or paint, you will need to decrease the amount of pure color in the mixture as you increase the white. A gradation of five to ten steps from the darkest to the lightest value is sufficient. The value difference between each step should be consistent, as in Fig. 3-1.

The degree of value difference between successive steps in the light half of the gradation should be approximately equal to the degree of value difference between steps in the dark half. The light and dark

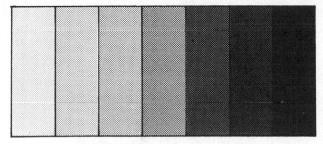

Figure 3-2. A seven-step gray scale. Notice that the value difference between steps 4 and 5 (light-to-dark sequence) is greater than the rest of the value contrasts in the gradation.

contrasts created as each value is placed next to another should also be consistent throughout the length of the scale. Too strong a difference between any two consecutive values will indicate a missing value and break the gradation, as shown in Fig. 3-2.

After you have worked out value gradations in several colors, compare corresponding colors from your fabric collection with those in the scales. Compare printed fabrics as well as solids. Try to look at printed fabrics not only as figured geometrics and florals but also as textured fields of color. Notice where different fabrics match values on the scale. This will give you a good idea of the relative position of your fabric on a value scale. After you've made the above comparison, group your fabric colors by corresponding value. Your value preferences and prejudices, if any, should become immediately apparent.

AN EXERCISE IN VALUE CHANGE

Just how relative value is becomes clear when we complete the next exercise. You will need to work with cut paper or solid fabric.

Choose two colors, one a light value and the other dark. They may be two strongly different values of the same color or contrasting values of different colors. The paper may be up to 9 in. by 12 in. (23 cm by 30.5 cm), and the fabric can be cut or folded to that approximate size. Now choose a third color or value from which two 2-in. (5-cm) or 3-in. (7.5-cm) squares will be cut. Do not use white or black. Place the small squares at the center of each of the larger color fields. The squares should no longer appear to be the same value. The square on the lighter ground should appear darker in value than its twin on the darker ground. Three distinct values are juxtaposed but four distinct values are perceived. Try several different colors in turn against your grounds until you find a combination that displays the value change most dramatically.

41   This exercise is demonstrated in neutral values in Fig. 3-3 and in the

Diagonal Log Cabin samples in Plate 35. Figure 3-4 demonstrates this same phenomenon by making two different values appear to be the same.

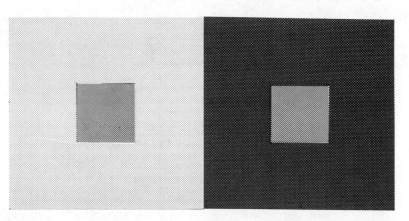

Figure 3-3. A demonstration of value change. The center squares are the same value of gray, made to appear different because of the contrast of the grounds on which they are set.

Figure 3-4. Two different values made to appear as one. The small rectangles at the bottom of the diagram show the actual values of the center squares relative to each other.

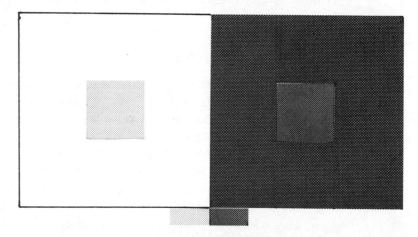

To the quiltmaker who might feel constrained by the occasionally limited range of fabric color available, the phenomenon demonstrated in the above exercise should suggest that fabric color limitations are themselves relative.

The value scales worked out above were monochromatic value gradations. Each represented a series of light and dark values of a single color.

Monochromatic value gradations can be used effectively to suggest a sense of space in a two-dimensional surface. The darker values appear to recede from the surface while the lighter values advance and even seem to rise off the surface. This spatial illusion can be emphasized by a corresponding size gradation in the value sequence. In Fig. 3-5 the white rectangle is closest to us, and as the values darken and reduce in size, they move away from us. This illusion is reinforced by the reverse progression in the background.

In Fig. 3-6 the intervals moving from light to dark get progressively smaller, so that the outer edges of the image are distorted and seem to pull inward just above and below each black stripe. The nar-

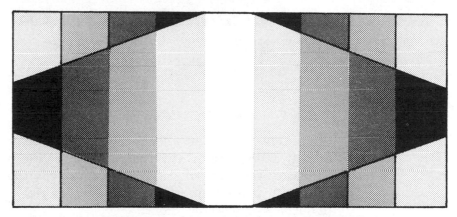

Figure 3-5. Combination value and size gradations help to create spatial illusions.

Figure 3-6. Value and size gradations cause the top and bottom edges of the scale to squeeze inward at the darkest steps.

row interval of black pulls the eye back behind the picture plane, defying the flatness of the image.

We see the reverse phenomenon in Fig. 3-7. The progression from wide black band to narrow white stripe causes that white to push forward on the picture plane. Just above and below the white bands the boundaries of the image seem to bulge out. In addition, the diffusion of the white with the wider gray bands to either side of it causes the white intervals to seem luminous. They appear to project light from within.

Figure 3-7. Here the white step in the gradation seems to move forward, causing the gradation to appear to bulge outward at those steps.

POLYCHROMATIC VALUE GRADATION

The true monochromatic value gradation involves a range of values of only a single color. It is spare and less expressive than the polychromatic value gradation. The latter affords the opportunity to work with subtle contrasts of color that can give a richness difficult to obtain with one color alone.

The harmonious progression of the polychromatic gradation depends on our recognition of the order in which colors are related. This order is represented in the color wheel and depends on the three primary colors. Since yellow and blue mixtures produce greens, it follows that in a natural sequence greens are located at intervals between yellow and blue. As a green becomes bluer, its position in that sequence moves closer to blue.

Polychromatic value gradations involving a limited number of adjacent colors may give a monochromatic impression. For example, a very light yellow green through to a dark blue-green will give a generally green impression.

We can, on the other hand, move completely around the spectrum, beginning with a light yellow and moving through light values of orange and red to pure violet and on through darker values of blue to the darkest green. The progression not only moves through color changes but also moves through a temperature change.

Both monochromatic and polychromatic value gradation scales are shown in Plate 33. The polychromatic gradation moves from green through blue-green and blue-violet to violet and red-violet.

It is extremely difficult to arrange a polychromatic gradation that does not follow the natural color order. Intensity is heightened when a color is placed outside of its hue and temperature range. In attempting this kind of integration the use of neutral grays can be helpful.

Maria McCormick-Snyder has used polychromatic value gradations effectively in *Log Cabin Variation* (Plate 17). The blues and blue-greens in the narrow bands create a "sunshine and shadow" illusion that pulls the eye into receding space. At the same time, the warmer progressions emphasize the large circular shapes that seem to move out from the surface. The horizontal and vertical black and white lattice strips, however, anchor these forms to the surface and help create a tension that energizes the surface.

COMPLEMENTARY COLORS

THE ADDITIVE FUNCTION

Each color lies opposite its complement on the color wheel. Complements are opposites in regard to temperature, and also in regard to the subjective responses they bring about. While orange is hot and fiery, an aggressive color that, when pure, assaults the eye with its radiance, blue is cool and refined, offering an atmosphere for reflection and quiet. Yellow is extremely bright and calls attention to itself through its lightness, while violet is dark and subdued, changing its character fluidly as it is placed in different color contexts.

As quiltmakers, we are especially interested in what happens to color when it is placed in different environments. We work with prepared colors, and as a result do not have the unlimited color range available to the painter. In certain instances it becomes necessary for us to change the appearance of those colors we do have, either intensifying them, reducing their brilliance, altering their temperature, or changing their hue.

Complements can be used to intensify one another. Intensity is the visual strength of a color. A pure red surrounding an equally pure green will intensify the greenness of that green. Red-violet will make yellow-green appear brighter and cooler than it does as an isolated pure color. A light value of yellow will appear almost weightless against an equal value of violet.

One noticeable result of the juxtaposition of two complements of equal value is the creation of a fine gray vibration at the edges of the two colors. The eye blends the two colors to create the suggestion of a neutral gray boundary. The visual sensation can be uncomfortable but is reduced once the values of the colors are no longer the same.

In the absence of the opposite color, any color will produce the impression of its complement. If you focus on a green swatch of fabric for a minute or so and then close your eyes, a red image will appear in the mind's eye. This afterimage also helps to explain the cancellation that occurs at the boundaries of two adjacent complements.

The complement of a color can also be used to alter the colors adjacent to its opposite. For example, a blue-green can be made to look more blue than green by setting it in an orange field. Red-violet will appear more violet than red when surrounded by yellow. Yellow-green will seem greener when set against red.

This effect of color intensification can be realized along the full length of the value scale, providing the opposing colors are approximately equal in value. A dark value of red-orange appearing as a deep reddish brown can be made redder by contrasting it with a dark value of pure green. A pale aqua will seem more green than blue when set against a pink of equal value.

The color interactions which occur when complements or near complements are contrasted are positive, or additive. They emphasize the character and personality of a color, and they intensify our own response in turn. When we want to create a feeling of pulsating life, energy, or intense surface activity, complementary contrasts are invaluable tools.

ADJACENT COLORS

THE SUBTRACTIVE FUNCTION

A pure blue-green can be made to appear more green than blue by placing it against a pure blue background. A light value of red-violet will seem cooler and more violet when surrounded by an equal value of red-orange. It can be made to appear warmer and more red when placed against a violet or blue-violet of equal value. When juxtaposed, colors subtract themselves from admixtures of which they are a part.

The activity of color subtraction can effect temperature and intensity changes as well as hue changes. Yellow-green will have some of its characteristic coolness reduced when set against green, and will appear more yellow. Against blue-green those changes will be heightened. That same yellow-green will display an increase in intensity if the green or blue-green are dark values. A dark value of red-violet will seem more violet in hue if placed against a deep red-brown.

Both the additive and subtractive functions of color demonstrate that a color can be a certain hue, value, and intensity in physical reality but at the same time can be made to appear different. This variability is called *simultaneous contrast*. An understanding of how these reversible influences can be effected is important to the quiltmaker working with a limited range of fabric colors.

AN EXERCISE IN SIMULTANEOUS CONTRAST

Choose from your fabric or colored paper collection a color other than one of the primaries. From this, cut five squares, each approximately 2 in. by 2 in. (5 cm by 5 cm). Set one aside on a white ground. This will be your constant and will act as a reference point.

Set each of the remaining squares against a different ground, attempting in the process to change value, intensity, temperature, and hue. You should strive to make the changes as dramatic and obvious as possible, taking into account the limitations imposed by the color selection you have before you. The best source of illumination for working out this type of color problem is reflected daylight; artificial light, as well as direct sunlight, will alter your perception of the color. You should be able to achieve the desired results, however, under any uniform light. As you make comparisons, stand away from the colors and try observing them all at once, rather than shifting your gaze back and forth between them. The relative ease or difficulty that you encounter in trying to effect these changes will depend in part on the character of the color you choose to alter.

COLOR TEMPERATURE

We have already seen how color temperature can be manipulated through the effects of simultaneous contrast. Temperature is one of the most relative characteristics of color, and hence one of the most variable. It is also perceived quite differently from person to person.

In a large group there will seldom be complete agreement on the respective temperatures of a given set of colors.

Greens are traditionally thought of as cool colors, and in pure form do have an inherent coolness. Blues likewise are thought of as cool colors, while reds and oranges are distinctly warm colors in their pure form, seen against white. Once a color is set against another, temperature becomes highly variable.

Temperature differences within a single hue range can be recognized most easily. A selection of six different reds, for instance, will reveal some to be cooler than others. A half dozen violets can likewise be differentiated. In turn, each of those reds and each of those violets can have its respective temperature modulated by being placed in other settings.

SPACE

Color temperature plays a critical part in the creation of an expressive quilt surface. It is also important in suggesting spatial illusions in the two-dimensional pattern. Traditionally, cool colors are thought to recede, and warm colors to advance. While these effects themselves are also variable (warm colors can be made to recede, while cools can advance, as in Plate 12), the basic principle can be employed to give depth to a surface design.

Black is the darkest color and can be made to recede furthest from the picture plane. Small spots of black appear to be figures in a white field. On the other hand, black can occupy the same plane as white, in which case there must usually be a precise balance and tension holding the two colors in that plane. We cannot determine which is the figure and which is the background, for there is a constant interchange between the two. When black is extended to become the field, white shapes become figures floating out in front of it, as in Fig. 3-8.

The spatial illusions can be heightened by the use of overlap. In Fig. 3-8, the small white stars run to the edges of the black field, joining with the white page. The page here becomes the picture plane, and the black rectangle is thus pushed behind it.

Proportion and overlap become key elements in the creation of spatial illusions on a two-dimensional surface. Progressive gradations in sizes of shapes, as in the Log Cabin variation shown in Fig. 3-9, can suggest volume as well as literal form. In this example, the form suggested is architectural. The pyramids seem real, and move out into space much as they would were they actual three-dimensional forms.

Overlap combined with value gradation gives the feeling that indi-

Figure 3-8. Black-and-white figure-ground relationships. In the diagram at top, the black stars may also be interpreted as holes in a white plane. At center, the star and pinwheel figures have an equal exchange value. The stars in the bottom arrangement become white figures in a dark, receding space.

Figure 3-9. Log Cabin variation creating a pyramid illusion.

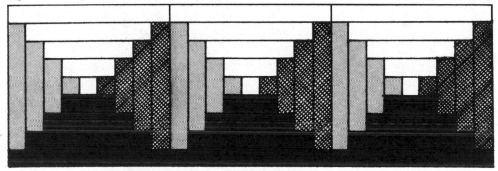

vidual figures are floating in space, flattened against planes that seem to be at different distances from one another. In Fig. 3-10, the smaller and lighter planes seem to advance toward the viewer. This illusion can be intensified by using a polychromatic value gradation in this arrangement. The cooler and darker colors in the gradation can push the larger planes further back in space, thus making the smaller planes in warmer, lighter values seem to move forward.

49

Figure 3-10. The gradation both in size and value of each of these planes causes the larger to recede and the smaller to advance.

TRANSPARENCY

Spatial illusions in the quilt surface can be heightened by the use of transparency. This is an effect in which two or more colors (or planes) overlap to produce additional colors. One of the colors seems to be behind the other, and their overlap is represented by a mixture of the two, producing an intermediate hue as well as an intermediate value (see Fig. 3-11).

The darker value will appear to occupy a plane behind the lighter, and this distance between the two can be intensified by juxtaposing a warm and a cool color. As discussed in the section on polychromatic value gradations, the transition from warm to cool can be effected smoothly through the use of a neutral gray.

You can use transparency systematically to suggest actual space or volume within a cubic form, as in Fig. 3-12. On the other hand, you

Figure 3-11. Transparency and overlap combining to create a spatial illusion.

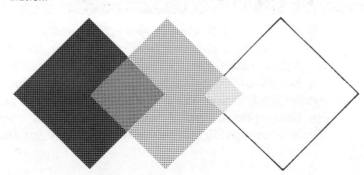

50

can use it randomly to create an indeterminate space on the two-dimensional surface.

In *Moonshadow* (Plate 15) I wanted to suggest a space that was less literal than that represented in the quilt *Aurora* (Plate 10). Forms twist and turn irregularly, and occasional overlaps of value or color or both determine whether a grouping of shapes is interpreted as figure or ground. The most active organization in the quilt is dependent on light and dark contrasts that set up a series of fluid and continuous diagonal curves.

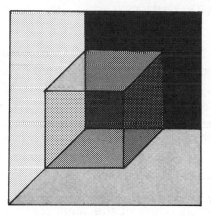

Figure 3-12. Transparency used to create a space and volume illusion.

THE EXPRESSIVE FACTOR

Although it's important that artists understand the physiology of color and of two- and three-dimensional design, it's also important that they not be governed by it in their work. A well-composed painting in pleasing colors, or a nicely proportioned covered jar, or a meticulously executed quilt color-coordinated to the furnishings of the room in which it is used will not necessarily contain that spark of life that reveals an intent beyond simply satisfying the so-called rules.

In working with fabric colors we as quiltmakers and designers must not only refer consciously or subconsciously to theoretical color interactions but must also respond intuitively and spontaneously to fabric color juxtapositions. The method of the educated guess comes into play here. Knowing that this or that effect might occur between certain colors, can I get the feeling I'm after by exaggerating that contrast, or by diminishing it? Can I integrate this piece of fabric by rearranging those others? How does this fabric look against that, and would one be diminished without the other?

It's important that every stitch taken in a quilt be either function-ally or aesthetically necessary, or both. Indiscriminate quilting, done just for the sake of saying "Look how much endurance I have!" di-minishes rather than enhances the surface. It's just as important that every piece of fabric be critical to the wholeness of the surface. Every spot of color introduced should relate, however indirectly, to every other piece. To effect this kind of unity takes a willingness to be directed as much as to direct.

A SPECTRUM OF CONTEMPORARY QUILTS

In her work, Nancy Crow typifies the artist who determinedly pursues a vision while responding flexibly to the limitations of the medium and the technique. Her quilt *Matisse Plain* (Plate 16) is a vivid collec-tion of warm and cool color contrasts. Darker values of color are or-ganized in the outer band in each of nine square repeats. These appear to contain in a shallow space the smaller and lighter squares. We revel in individual contrasts as we probe the different areas in the surface, yet we are always aware of the integrity of the whole.

In *February Study 2* (Plate 20) the artist plays with the picture plane more aggressively. Each of the value gradations is split so that colors change or light and dark progressions are reversed. Although tied to the central image, the large checkerboard triangles in the outer borders seem to loom out from behind the central square, pushing that area forward. The rust and black curves in the corners, split by color and value from the circles to which they belong, recede furthest from the picture plane.

March Study (Plate 22) amplifies the effects of the split value gra-dation. A large central square appears, with subordinate squares at each of its corners. The predominance of light values in the progres-sion causes the wide black stripping to become latticework through which we look at a lighter background.

In Beth Gutcheon's *The Goose Is Loose* (Plate 28) triangles take leave of their roost and fly out across an intense red field. Here a color with which we don't normally associate strong spatial effects becomes deep space. This is largely because of the symbolic function played by the triangles and of the associations we make in response to the title.

In *Ivy Covered Wall* (Plate 12) the spatial activity of warm and cool colors is reversed. Here, the cool greens and blue-greens come forward while the warmer oranges and browns pull back behind the black lattice. This occurs largely because the representational image brings to mind the reality of green ivy growing in front of a warm brick wall. It is intensified here because of value differences between the warm and cool colors.

I structured the quilt *Aurora* (Plate 10) in part on an extended ordering of warm and cool contrasts, as well as on a light and dark progression from top to bottom. I concentrated warm colors largely in the curved bands, while setting cool colors in the areas that group as background. Within the bands, split value gradations and color contrasts exaggerate the complexity suggested by the twisting and turning of the forms as they move across the surface.

My concentration on dark values in *Dawn Nebula* (Plate 9) gives that quilt a more mysterious, reflective quality than *Aurora*. I intended to evoke a sense of illumination by moving to lighter values at the center of the quilt. Although it is not as buoyant and optimistic in feeling as the earlier quilt, I don't feel it is necessarily pessimistic; it is, rather, a look inward.

4 The Curved Seam: Design And Construction

The curved seam as design form offers a literal fluidity and an organic flexibility that cannot be achieved with the straight seam. Curved-seam images have the capacity to pull us more actively into and around the quilt surface. They become more sensual designs. They possess not only the visual shape and color appeal and the tactile appeal of the fabric, but also the emotional appeal of softened and rounded forms. With our eyes we follow the contours of the shapes in the design as we would feel with our hands the contours of a gracefully thrown bowl.

Historically, the curved seam is represented by a modest collection of block patterns, including the popular Drunkard's Patch and others such as Robbing Peter to Pay Paul, Grandmother's Fan, Melon Patch, Winding Ways, Double Wedding Ring, and Clamshell (see Fig. 4-1). These patterns were rendered as repeat block surfaces, and the blocks were generally arranged symmetrically. Although symmetry and uniformity resulted, this tended to interfere with the expressive nature of the curved seam. Nonetheless, these patterns had

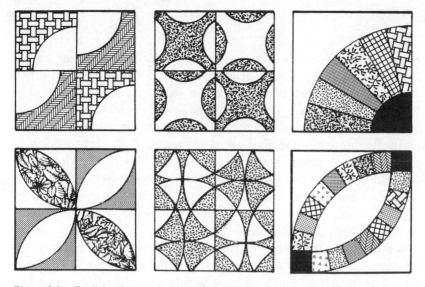

Figure 4-1. Traditional curved-seam block patterns.

a unique rhythmic and fluid quality not usually found in straight-seam quilts (see Fig. 4-2).

In this chapter we will work with modular design for the curved seam and will apply principles of asymmetrical surface composition to this form. Our emphasis will be on activating the rhythmic and fluid character of the curved seam and on transmitting that character to the quilt as a whole.

Figure 4-2. Comparison of curved-seam and straight-seam variations of the same arrangements.

Line is an integral part of the pieced quilt surface. The joining of two pieces of fabric along a seam produces line. In quilting, line is superimposed on the pieced image. This can be in the form of a broken dotted line (hand quilting) or a continuous line (machine quilting).

As we begin to explore surface design with the curved seam, we will concentrate on linear division of the repeat unit. Here we will be concerned not so much with the line itself, the positive element in the module, but with the intervals and shapes created between the lines. These negative spaces will become form when assigned roles as light or dark, warm or cool colors, with solid or printed, light-absorbent or light-reflective fabrics.

In working out the exercises that follow, it will be important for you to keep this in mind. You should be concerned with the grace or direction or length of a line or lines within a module. You must also give equal concern to shape interrelationships that are created because of the activity of those lines.

WHAT YOU'LL NEED

Several large sheets of paper will be useful for sketching out your block designs. You may want to rule a grid of 1½-in. (3.8-cm) to 2-in. (5-cm) squares across the surface of your paper. This provides you with a series of compartments for your sketches.

You will need a compass, preferably a screw-adjustable type. The squeeze-adjustable type of the dime-store variety is difficult to maneuver and cannot be relied on to hold to a setting if too much pressure is applied.

Several sheets of tracing paper will be needed to draft repeat block arrangements.

CURVED-SEAM EXERCISES

Work out a series of a half dozen to a dozen or so sketches in each of the linear arrangements suggested below. Try to vary each one as much as possible, exaggerating differences between each block design in a category. Certain groups of studies will lend themselves to variation more than others. Keep in mind that these are sketches for curved-seam piecing. Create pattern designs that can be pieced without extraordinary effort.

Equally Spaced Concentric Lines, Drawn with a Compass

Here the spaces between the curved lines are of equal width, although their lengths are graduated in size (see Fig. 4-3). The pivot point (that point where the metal point of the compass touches the paper) can be in a corner, but it can also be located anywhere outside or within the boundary of the block. These lines are parallel, and if extended beyond the limits of the block, will form circles.

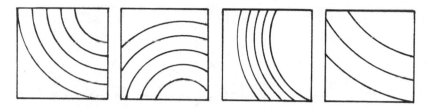

Figure 4-3. Equally spaced concentric lines, drawn with a compass.

Unequally Spaced Concentric Lines, Drawn with a Compass

In these units the lines remain parallel but the spaces created between the lines vary in width, as shown in Fig. 4-4. They may graduate proportionally from small to large, or the sequence may be irregular. The location of the pivot point is again variable.

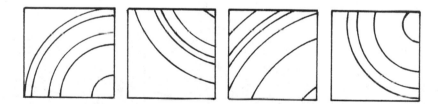

Figure 4-4. Unequally spaced concentric lines, drawn with a compass.

Lines Not Concentric But Not Crossing

Within the blocks shown in Fig. 4-5 no lines cross, although if the lines were extended beyond the boundary some would eventually cross. Compass-drawn lines no longer share a common pivot point. The curved forms may be arranged so that they oppose others, squeezing leftover space between them. Variations may be drawn freehand as well as with the compass.

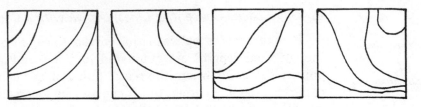

Figure 4-5. Compass- and freehand-drawn lines that are not concentric but do not cross.

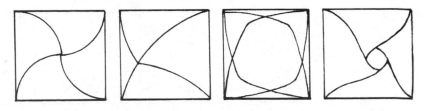

Figure 4-6. Crossing curves, corner to corner.

Crossing Curves, Corner to Corner

In these blocks (Fig. 4-6) any number of lines may be used, providing they each originate and terminate at a corner and cross another line or lines at some point in between. Draw these both with compass and freehand.

Figure 4-7. Crossing curves, center side to center side.

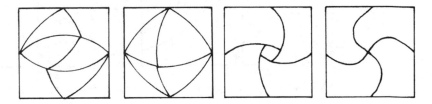

Crossing Curves, Center Side to Center Side

These lines begin and end at the precise centers of the sides of the block unit and cross others in between (Fig. 4-7). Draw several examples with compass, and others freehand.

Side to Side, To and From Uneven Points

In these units (Fig. 4-8) each line begins and ends at a different point along the outer boundary of the block. No two lines share the same points. Here the lines may be drawn with compass or freehand and may or may not cross.

Once you have a collection of sketches, you can begin experimenting with multiple arrangements of block designs.

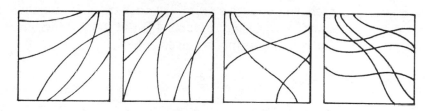

Figure 4-8. Lines moving side to side, to and from uneven points.

THE REPEAT SURFACE

The appeal of the curved-seam pattern lies not so much in the single block itself, but in what happens when that block is arranged in multiple. The meandering of the curved line and the interrelationship of the shapes created between blocks become the key elements in the surface design.

Using block patterns from the above exercises, you will now create repeat surfaces of curved-seam designs. You will find that the quickest and least complicated way of doing this is simply to trace the sketch in multiple with pencil or marker on tracing paper. After drawing a set of repeats of one block, you may wish to cut these apart and ex-

Figure 4-9. Multiple arrangement of a compass-drawn, equally spaced concentric line block design.

periment with rearranging them. When a satisfactory image is created, you can glue this to a sheet of paper.

Begin by choosing one or two of your sketches from each of the above exercises, and arrange each against itself at least nine (three by three) or up to sixteen times (four by four). You may wish to arrange each without turning in the first tracing, and then to cut the units apart as suggested. Figures 4-9 and 4-10 show blocks from Figs. 4-3 and 4-4 in multiple arrangement.

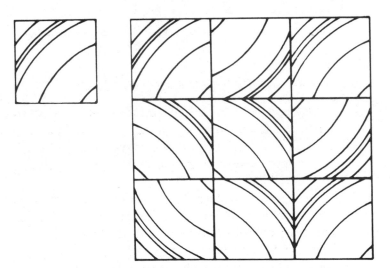

Figure 4-10. Multiple arrangement of a compass-drawn, unequally spaced concentric-line block design.

Next combine two different blocks in the same category in multiple arrangements (see, for example, Fig. 4-11). You will discover here that random distribution will create an image that seems less structured and will allow for a greater number of accidental line and shape combinations. Although compass-drawn curve patterns are geometric, you might try one as a contrast to a freehand curve block in a repeat structure.

Finally, complete a series of surface arrangements using in each two or three blocks selected from different categories. For example, you may use a nonconcentric, noncrossing block with a crossing-curve corner-to-corner design or with a side-to-side block in which lines move to and from uneven points (Fig. 4-12). You might wish to try equally spaced concentric lines with unequally spaced concentric lines and a block that is nonconcentric and noncrossing.

Figure 4-11. Multiple arrangement of two nonconcentric but noncrossing line blocks.

Obviously, in working out these exercises you will find that some of your block patterns are compatible, while others are not. Some will create fluid, lyrical surfaces, and some will appear awkward and contrived when arranged in multiple. You should feel free to make adjustments to a line or lines in a repeat in order to establish a better correspondence between blocks.

In curved-seam patterns, shapes assume gestures that are not typical of shapes in straight-seam design. As a result, the feeling of mo-

Figure 4-12. Multiple arrangement of a nonconcentric, noncrossing line block and a compass-drawn side-to-side block in which lines move to and from uneven points.

tion and activity is greatly increased in a curved-seam quilt. Curved shapes can appear to swirl and bend, to overlap and interweave in a much more natural way than can straight-edged shapes. This gives curved-seam patterns a representational quality that makes them seem less abstract than straight-seam designs.

AN EXERCISE IN SPONTANEOUS COLOR SELECTION

The fluidity of the curved-seam surface and the multiplicity of unexpected shapes that can be created within it are two reasons, among others, that seem to lend this form to the following exercise.

From the tracings of multiple arrangements that you have completed, choose one that seems successful or particularly interesting. Prepare a set (or sets) of templates for this pattern. You will need to complete at least sixteen blocks, four by four, for this project. I suggest a finished project size of 24 in. to 48 in. (61 cm to 122 cm). Size your templates accordingly. (A detailed treatment on making curved-seam templates follows in this chapter, along with sewing instructions.)

You will work out this surface without a prepared color sketch on paper. Any form of color organization you wish to develop must come about in response to the fabrics as you juxtapose them. You should attempt to use as many different fabrics as possible in this project. Although you will probably need to repeat certain fabrics, you should attempt to avoid repetition if your resources are substantial.

By studying your line drawing of the block (or blocks) in repeat, you may get a feeling that certain shapes function as figure, others as ground. Some shapes may group together in your eye because they repeat a certain direction or gesture or movement. The contrast of the straight horizontal and vertical grid (created by the joining of the blocks) with the curvilinear pattern may also suggest ways of organizing the color surface.

Light-and-dark contrasts, as well as warm-and-cool-color contrasts, can be used effectively, as we discussed, to give a feeling of space to the two-dimensional surface. You may decide to use one of these to help organize your surface. A value gradation through the piece, either from the center outward (and vice versa) or from top to bottom or side to side, may also enter into the design process.

Begin by choosing a fabric. Mark and cut it, and place it before you. With an adjoining template shape, cut a second piece of fabric in response to that first one, and lay it in place. Now choose a fabric for the next adjoining shape and lay it in place. Each new color selection will be based on what is already before you. Proceed in this fashion until you have resolved the entire design, and it is laid out ready to be sewn.

This is not a simple exercise. The challenge lies in using a large number of fabrics compatibly, organizing them intuitively, and completing the project without reference to a prepared plan other than the line drawing. You will find it extremely important to stand away from your work from time to time so that you can study the overall effect as it develops.

You may find that as you begin you have no perception of how best to organize the surface. As shapes are juxtaposed, this organization is developed and usually fully refined by the time you complete the project. At that stage, you may want to redesign earlier portions of the design. Be careful, however, that you don't alter the organizing structure as well.

The curved-seam quilt *Leaves* by Martha Maxfield (shown in Fig. 4-13) developed out of a spontaneous approach to color selection.

Figure 4-13. *Leaves* by Martha Maxfield. 1979. 36 in. by 36 in. (91.5 cm by 91.5 cm). Hand-pieced and hand-quilted cotton; polyester batting.

Figure 4-14. Untitled curved-seam study by Janie Burke. 1980. 45 in. by 45 in. (114 cm by 114 cm). Hand-pieced and hand-quilted silk, satin, velvet, and cotton; polyester batting.

Figure 4-15. Detail of curved-seam study by Janie Burke.

The freehand-drawn, side-to-side linear design is arranged to form a symmetrical pattern of softly waving forms. The blocks meet to form interesting negative shapes that define the space in which the curved forms float.

In the untitled curved-seam study in Figs. 4-14 and 4-15, Janie Burke chose two different curved-seam blocks and with them built an intense abstract surface. Forms are illuminated and shadowed in the interplay of lights and darks, and this gives a mysterious feeling to the image. The reflective nature of the satins and silks sets up dynamic contrasts with the light-absorbent fabrics. This helps to involve us more actively than we might expect if all the fabrics were plain-weave cotton.

THE CRAFT OF THE CURVED SEAM

All serious quiltmaking must reflect an intent to support honest surface design with the best construction possible. This is critical in work with the curved seam. We expect curvilinear images to have an elegance and fluidity not inherent in straight-seam work. This calls for precise workmanship that takes into account the individual nature of curved-seam construction.

DRAFTING THE CURVE

The average screw-adjustable compass will open to a radius of 4 in. to 6 in. (10 cm to 15 cm). This will produce a circle that is 8 in. to 12 in. (20 cm to 31 cm) in diameter.

For blocks larger than about 12 in. (31 cm) an extension bar is

Figure 4-16. Tools for drafting curved templates. The compass is screw-adjustable, and the extension bar alongside it can be used for marking larger arcs than the compass by itself can make.

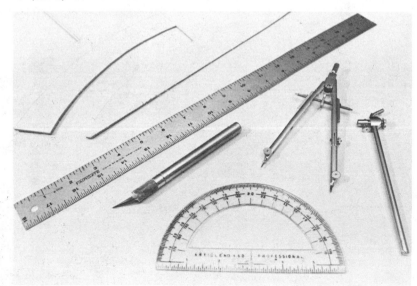

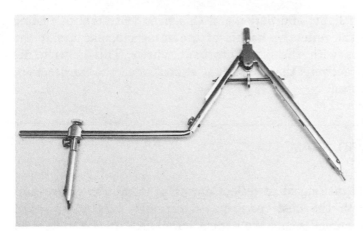

Figure 4-17. Compass with extension bar attached. The lead holder is removed from the leg of the compass and placed in the sliding carrier on the extension bar.

Figure 4-18. Holes drilled at 1-in. (2.5-cm) intervals in a wooden yardstick to be used as an improvised compass.

Figure 4-19. A push pin is held at the pivot point and a well-sharpened pencil is placed in a hole at the desired measure.

needed to draft larger curves. This is an attachment for the compass that increases the radius opening. Figure 4-16 shows a compass and an extension bar, and Fig. 4-17 shows the bar attached, with the graphite or lead holder attached to the sliding carrier on the bar.

When you need to draft larger curves, improvisation is the name of the game. I have had good results drafting arcs up to 6 ft (1.85 m) across by using a common wooden yardstick. Small holes can be drilled at 1-in. (2.5-cm) intervals along the center length of the yardstick, as in Fig. 4-18. A push pin or small nail is inserted near the beginning of the stick, and this acts as the pivot point. A well-sharpened pencil is held in one of the small holes at the desired measure, and the arc is drawn while keeping one hand on the pivot point and using the other to guide the pencil, as in Fig. 4-19.

THE TEMPLATE

By the time most quiltmakers attempt a curved-seam project, they have executed a number of straight-seam works, and have usually adopted one material or another for use in making templates. Some quiltmakers use lightweight cardboard such as posterboard, which they can cut easily with scissors. Other quiltmakers use thin plastic that they buy in sheet form in art or hobby shops and that can also be cut with scissors. Old X rays have turned up in some of my classes and have been used in making templates. There are undoubtedly hundreds of materials that could be employed successfully to service the quiltmaker's template needs. It is as much a matter of individual preference as every other aspect of the craft.

I have always used single-ply or double-ply illustration board. It is available in almost all art supply shops, is inexpensive, and produces durable templates. It cannot be cut with scissors, and this suits me because I find scissor-cut templates less accurate. I use an Exacto knife with No. 11 refill blades, but any stout-handled, razor-bladed knife with a straight, pointed blade could work as well. When using this tool along with a metal ruler to cut straight-edged templates, I find that I can get smooth, precise shapes. Handling these materials to make curved templates requires a bit more care, but for me they work as well.

Whichever material you use in making templates for curved-seam work, several considerations must govern how you prepare them. The first is that most curved fabric shapes are cut on the bias, and this necessitates careful matching of one shape to another. The curve of one shape must match the curve of the adjoining shape precisely. If not, the two pieces, once sewn, will not lie perfectly flat.

To solve this problem, notches are cut into the edges of each curved side on a template. After marking the shapes on the template material, notches are indicated at equally spaced points along each curve, as in Fig. 4-20. A short curved side may require only one or two notches; a longer side may require up to five or six or more. These notches are used to mark corresponding points on the curved fabric pieces.

If the curves are freehand-drawn, the notches should be spaced at intervals that appear to the eye to be approximately equidistant, as in Fig. 4-20. If the curves are drawn with a compass, it is more likely that you will be able to determine the exact center and the intervals equidistant from that. A protractor (Fig. 4-21) should be used for this measurement.

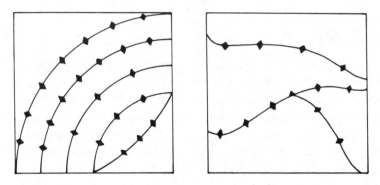

Figure 4-20. Notch placement indicated for compass-drawn and freehand-drawn blocks.

Figure 4-21. A protractor measures degrees on an arc. Note that in this example the base point (corresponding to the pivot point of the compass) is not on the bottom edge of the protractor.

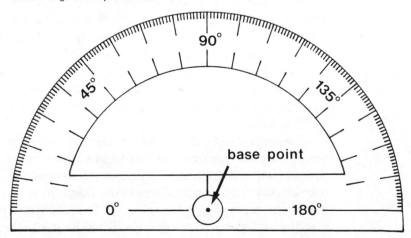

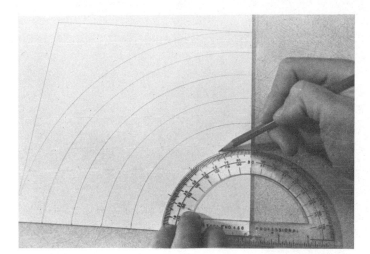

Figure 4-22. The protractor is used to mark equidistant points along the curved line.

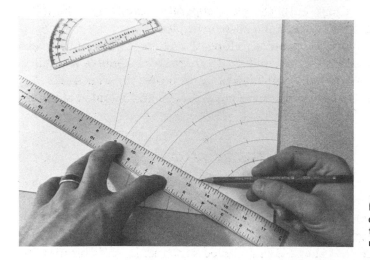

Figure 4-23. Corresponding points on each parallel line are indicated by ruling from the pivot point to the equidistant marks measured by the protractor.

The base point of the protractor is positioned so that it corresponds with the pivot point of the compass used in drawing the curves. If the curve is a full 90 degrees, you mark off the 22½-, 45-, and 67½-degree points at the circumference of the protractor. By ruling lines to and beyond these points from the pivot point, you mark off equidistant intervals on all curved seams in the repeat unit (see Figs. 4-22 and 4-23).

If you had no tapered points (see below) on any templates you would now be ready to cut the shapes. I always put a new blade in my knife when I'm ready to cut. This makes for a quicker, smoother job when a thick cardboard is used. I first score each curve; that is, I draw lightly over the line with the point of the blade, not trying to go through, as in Fig. 4-24. Once this groove is made, I repeat the

Figure 4-24. Scoring the cutting line between template shapes.

cutting several times until the piece separates smoothly. The initial cut helps to guide the blade in subsequent passes.

When separated, the notches along the curved sides of the templates can be cut, using the point of the knife to remove a small V-shaped piece from the template, as later shown in Fig. 4-27. Any straight sides of the template are cut with the knife guided along the edge of a metal ruler.

THE CASE OF THE TAPERED TEMPLATE

A second consideration applying only to hand piecing involves shapes in which the curve (or curves) taper to a fine point. This is most noticeable in corners of blocks in which the arc spans a 90-degree angle, as in Fig. 4-25.

The background shape B is a curved L shape, its ends terminating at a fine point. If the template were cut to exactly that shape, the

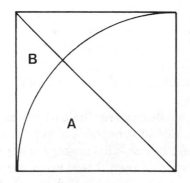

Figure 4-25. Templates for curves such as shape B must include reinforcement for the tapering curve.

actual ending points of the curve would be uncertain. In cardboard the template points would bend and quickly wear away. In plastic the fineness of the points at the ends of the template shape would make it very difficult to mark the shape accurately on fabric.

So that the full curve can be marked, an additional ¼ in. (6 mm) of template is included along both straight sides of that piece, as in Fig. 4-26. This equals the width of the seam allowance on those sides. The marking is made around the template on fabric, the notches being indicated as this is done (see Figs. 4-27 and 4-28). Before removing the template, however, it is shifted so that the extra ¼ in. (6 mm) of fabric is exposed. The straight sewing line is then marked with the edge

Figure 4-26. An extra ¼ in. (6mm) is added to the straight sides of the tapered-curve template.

Figure 4-27. Notches are cut into the curved edges of the templates.

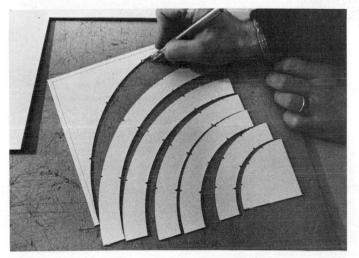

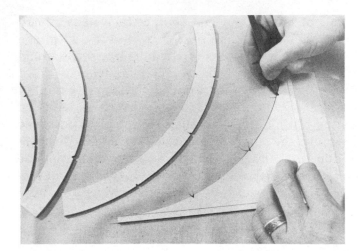

Figure 4-28. The notches indicate equidistant points where curved shapes will be pinned together.

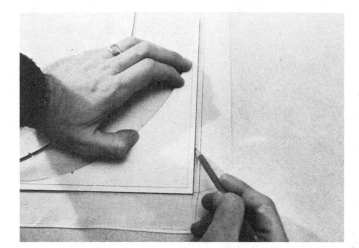

Figure 4-29. After the tapered-curve template shape is outlined, the template is shifted to expose the ¼-in. (6-mm) seam allowance on the straight sides. Sewing lines are then ruled by using the edge of the template.

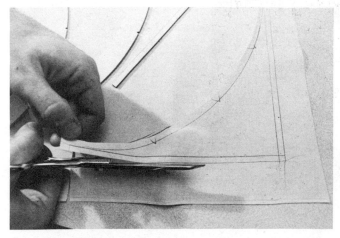

Figure 4-30. The seam allowance along the curved side of the tapered template shape is cut by eye. The outer straight line indicates the cutting line for the straight sides of the shape. The inner straight line is the sewing line.

of the template, as in Fig. 4-29. This line now meets the ends of the curved side.

When the fabric is cut, an extra ¼-in. (6-mm) seam allowance is added by eye to the curved side, but the straight sides are cut on the outer line (see Fig. 4-30).

MACHINE TEMPLATES

Since machine templates are made to include the ¼-in. (6-mm) seam allowance on all sides, the consideration we gave to tapering curves for the hand-piecing template is automatically taken care of here.

The most satisfactory method I've found for preparing machine templates (not only curved-seam, but straight-seam as well) begins with a careful drawing of the block pattern in finished size on graph paper. For the curved seam, this involves drawing the curves free-hand or with a compass and then indicating the notch points as described above. The shapes in the grid drawing are then cut apart carefully with scissors or with an Exacto. Each of these is then glued to the template board, as in Fig. 4-31. Enough space must remain between the shapes glued to the board to allow for the addition of the seam allowance measure for each shape.

A ¼-in. (6-mm) seam allowance is then marked around each shape. This can be done by measuring out from the edge of the paper shape

Figure 4-31. Preparation of machine templates. After the finished size shapes are cut from paper and glued in place, the seam allowance is added all around each shape.

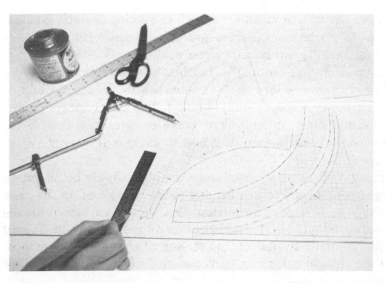

at very close intervals and then connecting these marks, as in Fig. 4-31. This outer line, which also indicates the cutting line of the template and of the fabric, should be precise and as near the contour of the original curve as possible.

Figure 4-32 shows sets of hand and machine templates for the same curved-seam pattern. Note the enlargement of the hand template along the straight sides with the tapering curves. This wasn't necessary on the machine template since the seam allowance took care of this.

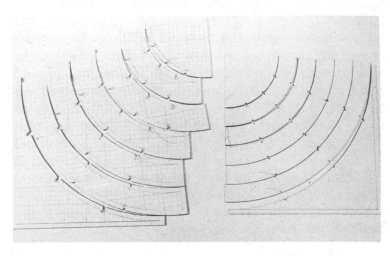

Figure 4-32. Comparison of hand and machine template sets for the same block design.

MARKING AND CUTTING THE FABRIC

All curves cut of woven fabric stretch to varying degrees. Whereas we attempt to minimize bias sides and stretch in straight-seam piece work, we use them to our benefit when working with curves.

When curves are cut on or near the bias of the fabric, it becomes much easier to ease one into another when sewing the seam. Clipping is seldom necessary, except perhaps in the case of very concave curves, or occasionally when an unbroken curve reverses direction. Since clipping weakens construction, it is best to use this device only when absolutely necessary.

Any straight edges on a curved-seam template should be placed on the straight grain of the fabric, parallel to the selvage, or on the cross grain, selvage to selvage. The longest side should be placed on the straight grain and any shorter straight side on the cross grain. Curved edges will automatically fall on the stretch of the fabric. Since most of or all the straight sides in a curved-seam design are the outer four sides of the module, all the stretch will be contained within the block. This will help prevent distortion in the overall surface.

Figure 4-33 shows a diagram for laying out assorted curved-seam template shapes. Fabric shapes for hand piecing should be spaced to allow for cutting with seam allowance. Straight sides of machine templates can be placed against one another, and certain curves on machine templates may fit inside their mirror images, and may thus share a common cutting line.

It's very important when marking curved-seam shapes on fabric to consider whether or not a particular template must be reversed (flipped over) on the back of the fabric. Many of these shapes have a particular direction which must appear right side up after the fabric is cut. You'll only need to cut one or two shapes incorrectly before you realize your error, but it's better to consider the possibility beforehand.

The cutting of hand-piecing shapes is done by eye, approximately ¼ in. (6 mm) from the sewing line. Machine-piecing shapes are cut on the pencil line, as accurately as possible. This cut edge acts as a guide for the seam allowance when machine sewing, and so any irregularity here will be transferred to the seamline.

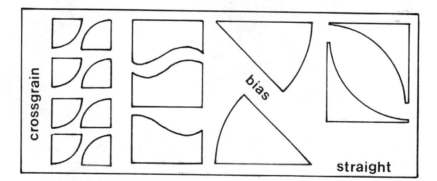

Figure 4-33. Diagram for laying out various curved-seam templates on fabric.

If you use satin-weave fabric in your hand piecing, cut the fabric with pinking shears. This prevents the fabric from fraying, which it can do unrelentingly if cut straight. In machine work, however, you will have to cut satins with regular dressmaker's shears and then handle with particular care when sewing. Cut velvets and velveteens with straight-edge shears also, and then use care in handling them when sewing. The pile on these fabrics will separate from the weave at the cut edge, but once these shapes are sewn and pressed, this shedding should not be a problem.

The most important aspect of the construction process for the curved seam is the pinning that precedes the actual stitching. Two matching curves must be exactly aligned and the fabrics eased one to the other so that there will be no puckering along the finished seams.

Begin by holding the two pieces of fabric with their right sides together, and pin through corresponding points at both ends of the seam. You will notice as you handle the fabric shapes for pinning that the curves do not reflect one another, but seem to go in opposite directions, as in Fig. 4-34. The curves must be shaped and fitted together, and this is what the pinning allows you to do. Proceed along the seam, setting pins through the sewing line at each notch.

Figure 4-34. Begin pinning at the end of the seam. Notice that the curved piece being attached turns in the opposite direction from those curves already sewn.

If there are spaces of a couple of inches (about 5 cm) or more between pins, it is helpful to pin here also (see Fig. 4-35).

When hand piecing the curved seam, adjustments of the two stitching lines can be made as you sew along the seam. If you notice that the two pencil lines do not align, you can adjust them slightly before proceeding.

Sew only on the pencil line. Do not sew through the seam allowances. When pressing, you will want the seam allowances to go in different directions. If they are sewn down, this won't be possible.

If you have had sufficient experience with straight-seam hand piecing, you will find the curved seam no more difficult. The only

Figure 4-35. Properly pinned seam ready to be hand-sewn.

adjustments you will make are in the additional pinning and occasional realignment of the sewing lines.

Special consideration must, however, be given to sewing curved-seam blocks together if they have tapering points in their corners. Two blocks are first pinned together. Any seam allowances approaching the corners must be turned toward the inner part of the block, as in Fig. 4-36. The sewing begins at the corners of the block where the tapered curve begins, and proceeds along the straight seam line. It is important that the needle avoid catching any fabric other than the two outermost pieces. Figures 4-37 and 4-38 show the back and front, respectively, of a seam joining two blocks where curves proceed from the corners.

Figure 4-36. Two blocks being sewn together, beginning at the tapered-curve corner. Notice that the seam allowance is turned down, out of the way of the needle.

After piecing each block, you will want to press it. Curved seams can be pressed in either direction, and several considerations will determine which way you press each seam. If, as described above, you are joining two tapered curves at a point, you will want to be sure that seams have been pressed away from the seam you will be sewing. If you have a series of concentric curves, you may want to press all seams in the same direction. If you are using a variety of fabric types, these may suggest which way to press. A heavy velveteen should probably not be pressed under itself; this would make the seam too bulky. A rayon or acetate satin will show a pressing mark on the surface if its seam allowances are pressed against it.

Experience will be the best guide in pressing. The main considera-

Figure 4-37. Back of two hand-sewn blocks, joined and pressed.

Figure 4-38. Front of hand-sewn blocks, showing how tapered curve disappears into a fine point.

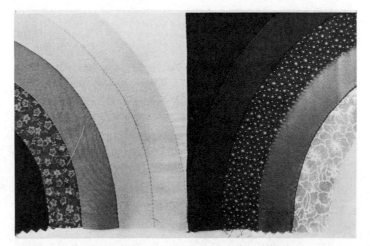

tion should be neatness of appearance. Press first from the back side of the work, distributing the seam allowances as necessary. Then press from the front side, using a pressing cloth to protect the fabric surface.

MACHINE PIECING THE CURVED SEAM

The curved seam may be sewn successfully by machine. Although the sewing will be faster than by hand, it will not be as fast as sewing a straight machine seam. Additional time and care must be spent in pinning two fabric pieces together, and careful attention must be paid to the seam guide and the edges of the fabric.

You should first pin through the fabric pieces wherever notch markings indicate corresponding points. Then pin generously between these points, as in Fig. 4-39. You will need to experiment to determine the minimum amount of pinning you'll need to produce a smoothly sewn seam. Start with more than you think you may need, and then reduce the number if you feel this won't affect the results. As you pin, be sure that the edges of both pieces of fabric align perfectly. Handle these pieces gently to avoid stretching them out of shape.

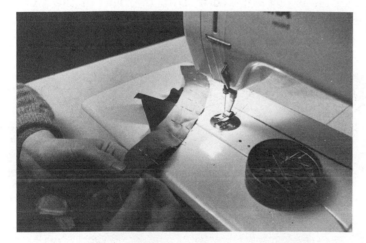

Figure 4-39. Pinning the curve for machine piecing.

Once the seam is pinned together, you can begin sewing, using about twelve to fourteen stitches to the inch (or 2- to 2.5-mm stitch length). Proceed slowly, removing pins as you come to them (see Fig. 4-40). Although some machines are capable of sewing over pins at slow speed, doing so requires caution. Should the needle hit a pin, the point of the needle will almost certainly be damaged, and this

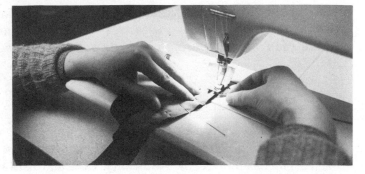

Figure 4-40. Pins are removed as the sewing proceeds. The edge of the presser foot is aligned with the edge of the fabric.

can affect the stitching in obvious ways. In some instances the needle will break, requiring an inconvenient pause to insert a new one and rethread. The biggest danger is that the sewing machine mechanism may be damaged by the sharp jolt of the needle hitting a pin.

Sew a ¼-in. (6-mm) seam, gauging this by the alignment of the fabric edges with the seam gauge on the machine. Most machines have seam gauges etched into the plate below the needle, as in Fig. 4-41. On some machines, the straight-stitch presser foot acts as the ¼-in. (6-mm) gauge. If your machine has no gauge, tape one onto the needle plate, so that its edge is just ¼ in. (6 mm) to the right of the point where the needle enters the base, as in Fig. 4-42.

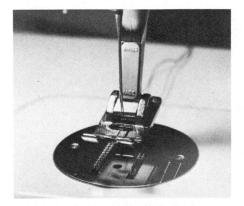

Figure 4-41. Seam guide etched into the needle plate of a modern sewing machine.

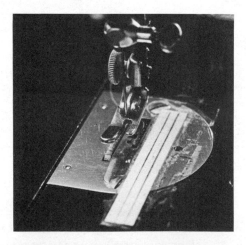

Figure 4-42. Improvised seam guide is a paper ruled in 1/8-in. (3-mm) intervals and taped in place on the needle plate. The left edge of the paper is 1/4 in. (6 mm) from where the needle enters the plate.

As with straight-seam machine work, curved seams must be pressed before they can be joined to a crossing seam. Seams may be pressed open in machine work, as in Fig. 4-43. This reduces bulk at matching joints.

Tapered curves at the edges of adjoining blocks are handled as any other machine seam. Since seams are pressed open, sewing begins at one corner and proceeds precisely ¼ in. (6 mm) from the straight edge of the fabric.

Figure 4-43. Back of machine-sewn curved seam blocks, showing seams pressed open.

Figure 4-44. Front of machine-sewn blocks. Compare these with the hand-sewn blocks in Fig. 4-45.

Figure 4-45. Front of two hand-sewn blocks.

Compare Figs. 4-44 and 4-45. In Fig. 4-44 the shapes and the blocks were sewn together by machine. In Fig. 4-45, the sewing was done entirely by hand. If sewing is precise, either technique will produce well-crafted results.

A GALLERY OF CURVED-SEAM QUILTS

Janie Burke approaches curved-seam design with a characteristic sense of humor and abandon. In *Rainbow Sherbets* (Plate 5) forms twist and turn and bounce off one another as they seem to try to escape from the square modules that contain them. The free-hanging curved forms surrounding the center of the quilt seem sober and controlled by comparison. In their regular placement and relative similarities to one another they recall strings of paper dolls, here guardians of a surface frosted with sherbet flavors old and new. This curved-seam quilt was hand pieced by the English Paper Patchwork method. Each fab-

Figure 4-46. *Fruit Slices* by Janie Burke. 1979. 60 in. by 87 in. (152.5 cm by 221 cm). Hand-pieced and hand-quilted silk, satin, and polyester; wool batting.

Figure 4-47. Detail of *Fruit Slices* by Janie Burke.

ric shape was first basted over a paper foundation and then whip-stitched to adjoining shapes.

In *Fruit Slices* (Figs. 4-46 and 4-47) these curved forms are fractured even further, dancing across the surface in a celebration of shape and color. The two angled corners increase this sense of movement and activity. Small geometric accents introduce unexpected surprises in the surface—the arrangements of triangles, the sawtooth and stripe borders, and the small pinwheel in the upper left. Something of "forbidden fruit" is also conveyed in this surface. Perhaps it is in the use of subtle pastels and flesh tones or in the recklessness with which the curved forms connect and disconnect. However it is suggested, it makes for a very original and expressive surface.

Nancy Crow uses curved seams as part of both *February Study 2* (Plate 20) and *March Study* (Plate 22). In both quilts sets of concentric curves are used to support value gradations that enhance the sense of spatial depth in these surfaces. In *February Study 2* these forms become medallions dominating the four corners of the quilt, and at the center they suggest newly opened flower forms. In *March Study* the curves grow out of neutral gray and tan background gradations to become intense red, blue, and green clusters defining flat planes that seem to be floating in front of the neutral background.

In *Aurora* (Figs. 4-48 and 4-49 and Plates 10 and 11) I set out to create a multicolored surface in which bands of color fracture the light that grows out of or is reflected by the quilt surface. Two repeat modules, one a soft S curve and the other a quarter circle, are arranged

Figure 4-48. *Aurora* by the author. Copyright 1978. 96 in. by 108 in. (244 cm by 274 cm). Hand-pieced and hand-quilted cotton, satin, and velveteen; polyester batting.

Figure 4-49. Detail of *Aurora* by the author.

asymmetrically on the surface. Each of these repeats is divided across the diagonal of the block, corner to corner, and then further subdivided into concentric bands of equal width. To set them apart as distinct forms, I concentrated warmer colors in the bands and juxtaposed these against cool colors in what became the background. Quilting echoes each of the curves, and where corners of blocks meet, sixteen-pointed stars or fractions thereof appear in quilting. An update of the traditional feather vine and wreath is rendered in quilting in the large triangular areas, an elongated triangle being used to replace the teardrop along the stem of the pattern.

Dawn Nebula (Plate 9) is one-quarter the size of *Aurora* and is a reinvestigation of the same two repeat modules. The light effect is now contained by a more mysterious rendering of the curved bands in dark, receding colors. Whereas I intended the first quilt to be a

Figure 4-50. *Suntreader/Polyphony* by the author. Copyright 1979. 60 in. (153 cm) diameter. Hand-pieced and hand-quilted cotton, satin, and velveteen; polyester batting. Collection of I.B.M. Corp.

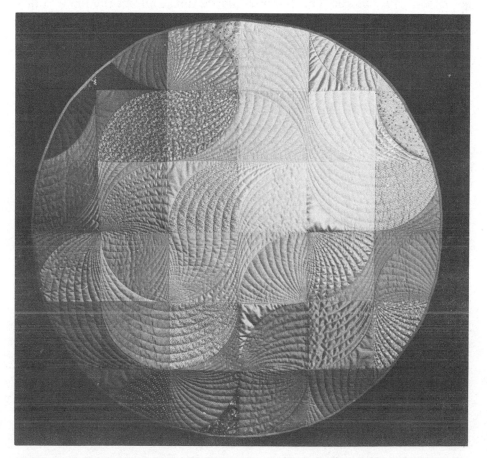

celebration of light and color, I wanted the smaller quilt to be a more reflective, introspective study with a more abstract, spiritual tone.

Moonshadow (Plate 15) represents a movement away from the complexity of the previous two quilts. Although I was still interested in the random arrangement of the repeat units, I wanted to establish a linear continuity in parts of the surface. The overall color composition was based largely on light and dark contrasts, and these help to set up that linear flow. Occasional color transparencies provide a sense of space. The title for this quilt was suggested by the flickering of lights and darks throughout the surface.

When I completed *Suntreader/Polyphony* (Figs. 4-50 and 4-51 and Plate 14), the quilt represented a departure on my part from the saturated colors that populated the previous works. The round form attracted me because of its more organic character, as well as the associations with natural and man-made objects that it suggests. In this case, the quilt is a specific reflection on the sun. The repeat module used in *Moonshadow* is simplified even further here with the elimination of the diagonal seam in the block. Each unit now consists of only two pieces. This minimal pieced image allows the linear quilting design to assume equivalent decorative status.

Figure 4-51. Detail of *Suntreader/Polyphony* by the author.

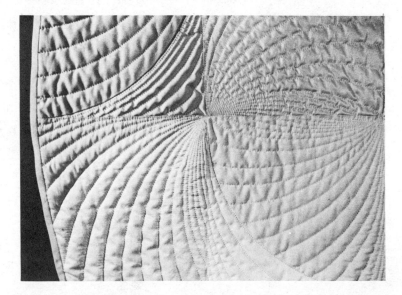

5 Strip Piecing The Quilt Surface

The technique of strip piecing (also known as Seminole patchwork) opens up an entire world of pieced-surface design that would be beyond the range of practical possibility in conventional pieced-work technique.

Strip piecing is the process by which long strips of fabric of varying widths are sewn together by machine to create, in effect, the yardage from which the surface will be designed. Having marked the shapes with ruler and pencil or with templates, the quiltmaker then cuts them from this strip-pieced yardage. The shapes are then resewn to create the complex surfaces that characterize the strip quilt.

THE TECHNIQUE OF STRIP PIECING

The most important tool in strip piecing is the sewing machine, and it must be in good working order. Be sure that it is clean and free of dust and lint buildup. The needle plate as well as the face plate of the machine head should be removed and any dust brushed out. Oil the

87

machine according to the manufacturer's instructions. If you haven't used your machine in a month or so, you should probably oil it. The more you use the machine, the less you'll need to oil it. Be sure to sew over a scrap of fabric before beginning, so that excess oil will be absorbed and won't soil your good fabric.

Start your work with a new sewing-machine needle. A burred or dull needle will affect the stitching. Be sure to select the needle size that corresponds to the type of fabric you are working with.

A good quality cotton-covered polyester thread should be used. If you're working with dark fabrics, choose a dark thread; with lighter fabrics use a light-colored thread. You may prefer to use a neutral, middle-value gray for all your strip piecing.

Be sure that your fabric shears are well sharpened. The entire length of each fabric strip must be hand-cut, and dull scissors make this twice the effort. Tearing the fabric strips is not recommended, unless accuracy is not one of your considerations. Test your scissors to be sure they cut smoothly the entire length of the blade, right to the tip. If not, have them sharpened.

Choice of fabric will probably be dictated by what you are currently working with. The easiest fabric to work with to achieve accuracy is 100 percent cotton broadcloth, followed closely by synthetic and cotton-blend broadcloth. Satins and other slick, shiny fabrics are the most difficult to handle in strip piecing. Your experience at the sewing machine will also influence your fabric choices.

MARKING AND CUTTING THE FABRIC

Anyone who does strip piecing will agree that marking and cutting the fabric strips is the tedious part. It must be done carefully and accurately, since the correct fit of all the pieces in a design will depend on how straight the edges of the strips were cut. It helps to anticipate the glory of the final result while preparing the fabric for sewing.

Strip lengths longer than 1½ yards (1.4 m) become unwieldy and therefore are not recommended. For large projects, fabric may be purchased in 1-yard (0.95-m) or 1½-yard (1.4-m) lengths. For smaller projects, 18-in. to 24-in. (45.7-cm to 61-cm) lengths will be suitable. If you prefer to cut the strips across the grain of the fabric as described below, your strip length will equal the width of the fabric.

Strips can be any width, depending on the proposed size of the final project. Widths finishing less than ¼ in. (6 mm) present the problem of interference by the seam allowances on the back side of the work. The widths of the strips should be scaled to the size of the shape that will be cut from them, as well as to the size of the whole project.

Quilts in Color

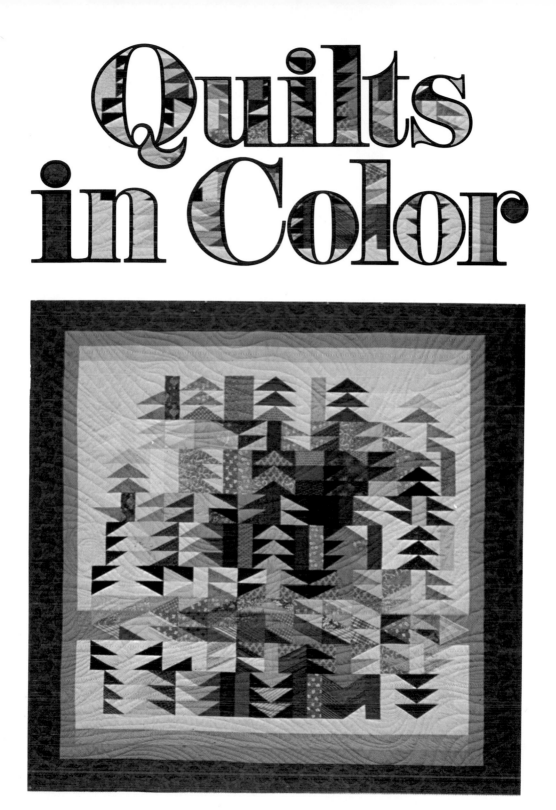

Plate 1
(above) *Fall's Island* by Nancy Halpern. 1979. 84 in. x 84 in. (213 cm x 213 cm).
Cotton and cotton blends; polyester batting. Hand-pieced and hand-quilted.
Photo courtesy of the artist.

Plate 2
(right) *Whirligig* by Virginia Anderson. 1979. 65 in. x 65 in. (165 cm x 165 cm). Hand-pieced and hand-quilted cotton, velveteen, corduroy; polyester batting.

Plate 3
(below left) *Aquarius Quilt* by Nell Cogswell. 1978. 84 in. x 84 in. (213 cm x 213 cm). Hand-pieced and hand-quilted cotton; cotton batting. Photo courtesy of the artist.

Plate 4
(below right) *Flying Carpet* by Nancy Halpern. 1979. 72 in. x 85 in. (183 cm x 216 cm). Machine-pieced, hand-quilted cotton and cotton blends; polyester batting. Photo courtesy of the artist.

Plate 6

(above left) *Farmscape Times Three* by Janie Burke. 1978. 89 in. x 89 in. (225 cm x 225 cm). Hand-pieced and hand-quilted satin, velvet, taffeta; cotton batting.

Plate 7

(above right) *Lightning Ranger* by Sunny Davis. 1979. 54 n. x 54 in. (137 cm x 137 cm). Machine-pieced and hand-quilted cotton; polyester batting.

Plate 8

(below right) *Boxes and Stars* by Peggy Spaeth. 1979. 72 in. x 72 in. (183 cm x 183 cm). Machine-pieced and hand-quilted cotton and cotton blends; polyester batting. Photo courtesy of James Coburn.

Plate 5

(above) *Rainbow Sherbets* by Janie Burke. 1978. 60 in. x 87 in. (152 cm x 221 cm). Hand-pieced and hand-quilted silk, satin, and velveteen; wool batting.

Plate 9

(right) *Dawn Nebula* by the author. Copyright 1979. 48 in. x 54 in. (122 cm x 137 cm). Hand-pieced and hand-quilted cotton, satin, and velveteen; polyester batting. Collection of Dual-Lite, Inc.

Plate 10

(below right) *Aurora* by the author. Copyright 1978. 96 in. x 108 in. (244 cm x 274 cm). Hand-pieced and hand-quilted cotton, satin, and velveteen; polyester batting.

(opposite page)
Plate 11
Detail of *Aurora* by the author.

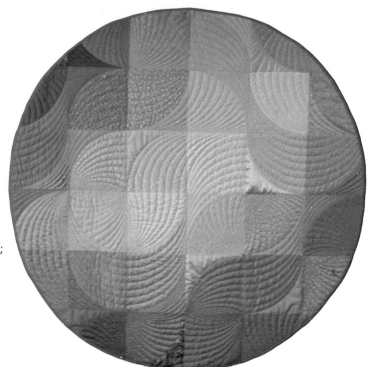

opposite page

Plate 12
(above left) *Ivy Covered Wall* by
the author. 1979. 48 in. x 48 in.
(122 cm x 122 cm). Machine
appliquéd and hand-quilted cotton;
polyester batting. Collection of
Tim James.

Plate 13
(below left) *Poppies* by the
author. 1979. 56 in. x 65 in.
(142 cm x 165 cm). Machine
Log Cabin; Pellon fleece batting.
Collection of I.B.M. Corp.

Plate 14
(above) *Suntreader/Polyphony*
by the author. Copyright 1979.
60 in. (152 cm) diameter. Hand-
pieced and hand-quilted cotton,
satin, and velveteen; polyester
batting. Collection of I.B.M.
Corp.

Plate 15
(left) *Moonshadow* by the
author. Copyright 1979. 80 in. x
100 in. (203 cm x 254 cm).
Hand-pieced and hand-quilted
cotton, satin, and velveteen;
polyester batting. Collection of
Dual-Lite, Inc.

Plate 16
(left) *Matisse Plain* by Nancy Crow. 1977. 68 in. x 68 in. (173 cm x 173 cm). Machine-pieced cotton blends; polyester batting. Hand-quilted by Velma Brill. Photo courtesy of the artist.

Plate 17
(below) *Log Cabin Variation* by Maria McCormick-Snyder. Copyright 1978. 73 in. x 73 in. (186 cm x 186 cm). Machine-pieced, hand-quilted cotton; polyester batting. Photo courtesy of the artist.

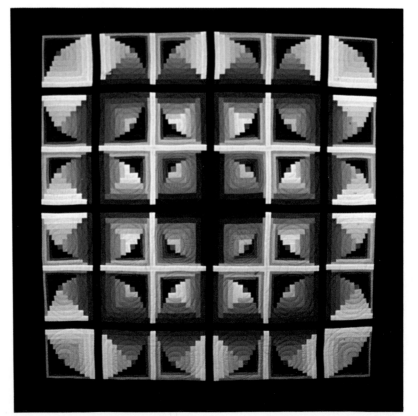

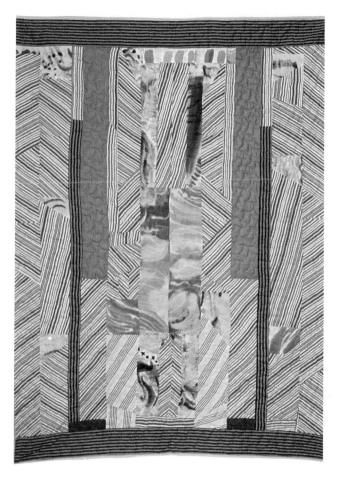

Plate 18
(above) *Wholeness* by Radka
Donnell-Vogt. 1979. 54 in. x 79
in. (137 cm x 201 cm). Machine-
pieced cottons. Machine-quilted
by Claire Mielke. Photo courtesy
of the artist.

Plate 19
(right) *Blue Metamorphosis* by
Françoise Barnes. 1979. 75 in. x
75 in. (191 cm x 191 cm).
Machine-pieced, hand-quilted
cotton blends; polyester batting.
Quilted by Bertha Mast.
Photo courtesy of the artist.

Plate 20

(above left) *February Study 2* by Nancy Crow. 1979. 60 in. x 60 in.
(152 cm x 152 cm). Machine-pieced cotton blends; polyester batting.
Quilted by Velma Brill. Photo courtesy of the artist.

Plate 21

(below left) *Newe II* by Nancy Crow. Copyright 1980. 72 in. x 72 in.
(183 cm x 183 cm). Machine-pieced cotton blends; polyester batting.
Hand-quilted by Mrs. Levi Mast. Photo courtesy of the artist.

Plate 22

(below) *March Study* by Nancy Crow. 1979. 80 in. x 80 in. (203 cm
x 203 cm). Machine-pieced cotton blends; polyester batting. Hand-
quilted by Mrs. Levi Mast. Photo courtesy of the artist.

Plates 23-27
Day Lily Series I-V by Beth Gutcheon. Copyright
1979. The series begins with *Day Lily I* (below)
and runs down the left column and then the right
to the end of the series, *Day Lily V.* Each quilt
is 23 in. x 25 in. (59 cm x 64 cm). Machine-
pieced, hand-quilted cotton; polyester batting.
All photos courtesy of the artist.

Plate 28

(below) *The Goose Is Loose* by Beth Gutcheon. Copyright 1979.
Machine-pieced, hand-appliquéd, hand-quilted cotton and cotton blends;
polyester batting. Private collection. Photo courtesy of the artist.

Plate 29
(top left) *Rainy Day Crocuses* by Nancy Halpern.
1979. 40 in. x 40 in. (102 cm x 102 cm).
Machine- and hand-pieced and hand-quilted
cotton; polyester batting.

Plate 30
(left) *Pansies* by Martha Maxfield. 1979. 30 in. x
30 in. (76 cm x 76 cm). Hand-pieced and hand-
quilted cotton and velveteen; polyester batting.

Plate 31
(top right) *Cactus* by Debra Hoss. 1979. 30 in. x
30 in. (76 cm x 76 cm). Machine-pieced, hand-
quilted cotton; polyester batting.

Plate 32
(above right) *Winter Cactus* by the author. Copyright 1978. 42 in. x 42 in. (107 cm x 107 cm).
Machine-pieced; hand-quilted cotton, satin,
velveteen; polyester batting. Collection of Mr. and
Mrs. John Middleton.

opposite page

Plate 33
(above) Color wheel with monochromatic and
polychromatic value scales.

Plate 34
(below) Asymmetrical block in four-color
compositions.

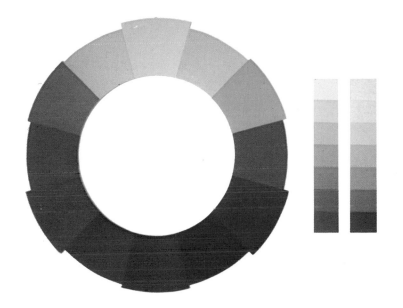

Plate 35
(above) Value change in clockwise-sequence Log
Cabin blocks and intensity change in opposite-
sequence Log Cabin blocks.

Plate 36
(below) Pineapple Log Cabin sampler by the
author. 1977. 24 in. x 24 in. (61 cm x 61 cm).
Cotton; hand-pieced.

 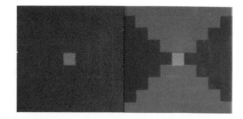

If you plan to cut strips along the straight grain of the fabric, you can measure the width of each strip from the selvage, as in Fig. 5-1. Mark off a series of points each the same distance from the selvage, and then connect these points with a straight line. This is your cutting line.

Figure 5-1. Strip widths being measured from the selvage.

Each strip must include seam allowance. If you wish the strip to finish 1 in. (2.5 cm) wide you must measure and cut it as a 1½-in. (3.8-cm) strip. If you need several strips of that same fabric, simply continue to measure down from each ruled cutting line until you have marked off the desired number. If you mark and cut parallel to the selvage, each strip will be on the straight grain and therefore will not stretch.

I have found that with certain broadcloths in blends of 65 percent polyester and 35 percent cotton, the strips, when sewn and pressed, pucker slightly along the seam, as in Fig. 5-2. If desired, this can be avoided by cutting these fabrics in selvage-to-selvage strips, or across the grain. This does make the fabric a bit harder to handle, however. The stretch on the cross grain can affect the marking, cutting, and sewing. Therefore, you should exercise additional care at each step.

The puckering can also occur as a result of incorrect thread tension adjustment. Consult your machine guidebook for instructions on tension adjustment.

You may prefer to use templates to mark the strip widths. These must be as wide as the finished size of the strip, plus seam allowance. A template for a 2-in.- (5-cm)-wide strip, for instance, will be 2½ in. (6.3 cm) wide. The longer the length of the template, the fewer times

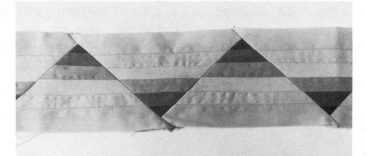

Figure 5-2. Puckering along seams.

you'll have to move it along the length of the fabric. You may already have several ready-made strip templates in the form of long rulers. A yardstick or meter stick that measures 1½ in. (3.8 cm) wide makes a perfect template for a 1-in. (2.5-cm) strip.

Since the stitching is done by machine, there is no need to mark a stitching line on the strip. The seam gauge on your machine will guide you in sewing a straight seam. It is critical, however, that the strips be cut straight.

It is very difficult to estimate how much strip length of each color to cut for a particular design. At first it is wise to prepare less than you think you'll need, in order to find just how many design pieces can be cut from a given length. With some experience, you will be able to estimate the rough number of strip lengths to cut to complete the desired pattern.

SEWING THE STRIPS

Use a stitch-length setting that will provide from ten to twelve stitches to the inch (per 2.5 cm). Pin two strips with their right sides together at regular intervals to keep their edges aligned.

Lift the presser foot and place the ends of the strips under the needle, aligning their edges with the seam guide. Take hold of the needle and bobbin thread ends, and pull out several inches of each. Drop the presser foot. Guide the needle down into the fabric by rotating the handwheel manually. If the thread ends are not sufficiently long and not held securely, they may easily become tangled around the bobbin case when you begin sewing.

Begin stitching, gently guiding the fabric under the presser foot with your right hand, and guiding it out behind the needle with your left. The problem of seam puckering that occurs with certain cotton and synthetic blends can be reduced by holding the strips taut as they are guided under the needle. Pay careful attention to the seam guide to assure that your seams will be straight.

Once you have sewn the strips, press the seams open. Press first from the back side of the piece, and then from the front. Be sure that all seam allowances lie perfectly flat.

When you have sewn and pressed a set of strips, you will notice that the top and bottom strips in a set are wider than those in between, as in Fig. 5-3. The outer strips have lost only one seam allowance, whereas the inner strips have lost both and are now at their finished widths.

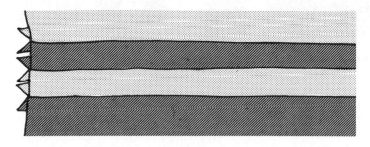

Figure 5-3. The outer strips in the pieced stripping are wider because of outer seam allowances.

MARKING AND CUTTING THE DESIGN UNITS

There are two possible approaches to marking the shapes that will be cut from the strip sections. The first is to measure and mark with pencil and ruler. The second method employs machine templates as in conventional pieced work.

Figure 5-4. Marking for square units on strip fabric.

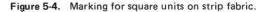

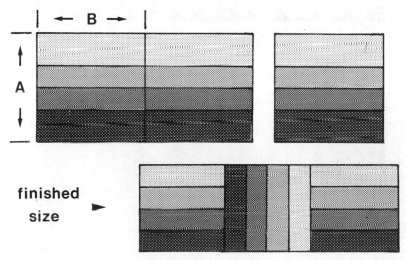

finished
size ▶

Since the pencil line is the cutting line, mark on the front side of the strip-pieced fabric. Marking on the back can be complicated by the large number of seam allowances.

Simple shapes that use the full width of the strip yardage can be ruled directly on the fabric. Squares are measured along the top and

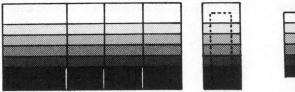

Figure 5-5. Marking for rectangular units on strip fabric.   **finished size** ↑

Figure 5-6. Triangular units cut from squares marked on the strip fabric. These can be grouped in a number of ways to create a variety of designs.

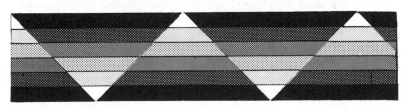

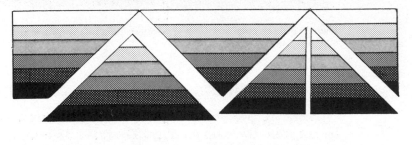

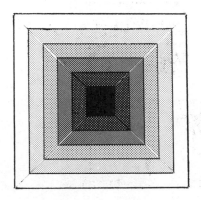
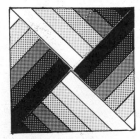

bottom of the strip section, at intervals equivalent to the width of the strip fabric, including the seam allowances (see Fig. 5-4). Rectangles are measured likewise, but you must add seam allowance when marking the top to bottom sides, as in Fig. 5-5.

Right triangles can be measured by marking off squares and dividing them in half on the diagonal, as in Fig. 5-6. It is important to be aware that seam allowances will reduce the size of the triangle considerably in the final sewing.

The use of strip piecing becomes much more flexible when templates are used for marking, much as they are used in conventional machine-pieced work. Templates that include seam allowance are prepared on the basis of a plan for the entire project. Shapes are then marked on the strip fabric without the need to give additional consideration to seam allowances.

The pieced work shown in both Figs. 5-7 and 5-8 is based on the use of templates to mark the desired shapes. In Fig. 5-7 four different triangular templates are employed for the strip piecing, along with an additional elongated triangle used for the solid white shape

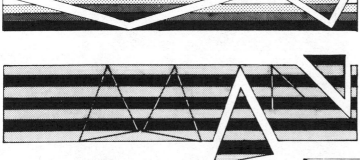

Figure 5-7. Four different triangular templates are used to cut the strip fabric. The sections are then arranged to form a symmetrical image.

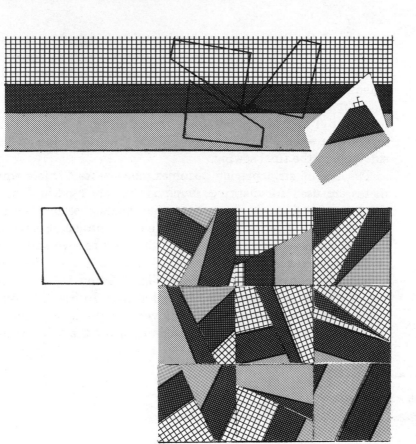

Figure 5-8. A single template shape is used to cut at random. The resulting patchwork image is asymmetrical.

Figure 5-9. Triangular sections are pinned so that their corners overlap. Seams will then join in the final result.

in the pattern. In Fig. 5-8 a single template is used to create an asymmetrical pattern reminiscent of late nineteenth-century crazy patchwork.

JOINING THE DESIGN UNITS

When you are ready to begin joining the various shapes cut from the strip-pieced fabric, proceed as you would for regular piecing. Place shapes with their right sides together and pin them to prevent shifting. If there are any seams that must join at corresponding points, pin these to assure exact alignment. Figure 5-9 shows two strip sections pinned together so that the seams will meet, as well as the completed section.

If you are joining several sets of the same shapes, sew these all in one sitting and then press the seams open. Press from the back side first, being careful that all seams lie flat. Then press from the front side.

The technique of strip piecing is relatively simple, and is a marvelously quick way to achieve some very complex images. Every step of the process, however, requires organization and careful preparation.

DESIGN FOR STRIP PIECING

As suggested above, the strip-pieced quilt surface can achieve a complexity beyond the range of practical application of conventional machine-pieced work. Strip piecing acts as an excellent foundation for working out interesting color interactions. It can also serve to heighten spatial illusions in the quilt surface.

SINGLE-WIDTH STRIPPING

The basic arrangement of fabric strips of equal width lends itself to value gradations because of its regularity. Figures 5-4, 5-5, and 5-6 demonstrate the use of value gradation in strip sections. By nature, these gradations suggest a three-dimensional space in the two-dimensional surface. Forms appear to be in front of or behind others. They can also appear to move out from or recede behind the picture plane.

Single-width strip sections work well as supports for light and dark color contrasts, as well as for temperature contrasts. Light strips alternating with dark ones create strip designs that have a very bold,

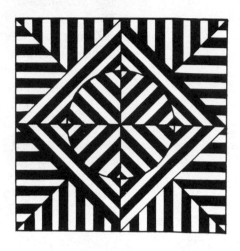

Figure 5-10. Single-width stripping for light and dark contrasts.

communicative quality. As illustrated in Fig. 5-10, the regular repetition of the contrast helps to create a strong surface texture when these strip sections are used extensively. Warm and cool color contrasts become by nature more expressive, and can energize the strip surface with strong, intense color vibrations. They can also be used to suggest a particular mood or evoke a particular viewer response.

MULTIPLE-WIDTH STRIPPING

Gradation in the strip-pieced fabric can also appear as a progressive size change in the strip widths. This width gradation coupled with a value gradation can exaggerate spatial illusions. Figure 5-11 illustrates the combined use of value and size gradations. Varied widths can also be arranged at random, as in Fig. 5-8.

USING STRIPES AND OTHER FIGURED FABRICS

Although most strip piecing has traditionally been done in solid-color fabrics, you can also use woven or printed stripes, printed florals

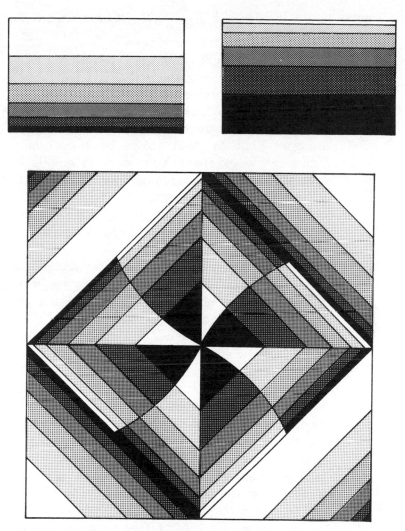

Figure 5-11. Graded-width stripping combined with a value gradation emphasizes spatial illusions.

and geometrics, or woven or printed plaids. Striped fabrics relate particularly well and can be used to increase the complexity of the strip surface design. Very fine stripes, too difficult to achieve in strip piecing, may be introduced by way of narrow printed or woven stripes.

Printed florals and geometrics should be used judiciously. Very busy prints can disguise the strip-pieced work if used in large amounts. These fabrics add visual texture to the quilt surface, and should be used to complement the textures already provided by the strip piecing itself.

The following exploration will introduce you to the design possibilities of strip piecing and will also suggest an approach to working out preliminary models for large-scale projects.

You will need an assortment of colored paper. Several packages of multicolored construction paper will offer you a workable selection. I suggest 12-in. by 18-in. (35-cm by 45-cm) sheets, as these will provide longer single strips. Your local art supply shop may have other colored papers that you can use in addition to the construction paper to broaden your color range.

You will also need paper-cutting scissors, a ruler and pencil, and a full roll or two of transparent tape. A lightweight cardboard can be used for making templates.

After cutting and taping together a number of strip sections on the basis of compatible color arrangements, you will cut from them the shapes needed to complete a symmetrical or asymmetrical block pattern. Keep in mind that you will be taping the strips edge to edge, and seam allowance will not be a consideration here.

The first strip section you will arrange is a single-width monochromatic value gradation. (See Chapter 3 for a detailed discussion of monochromatic gradations.) Begin by choosing any color that appeals to you, and then complete a four-value gradation of that color. Cut one strip of each value; each strip should measure 1 in. by 18 in. (2.5 cm by 45 cm). Tape these together from the back, along the full length of each seam. You will find it easier to cut short lengths of tape and place these end to end than to cut one long length. The finished strip section should measure 4 in. by 18 in. (10 cm by 45 cm).

The second strip section will contain a warm versus cool contrast of two colors. Choose the first color for this set from those in the completed gradation. Then select the contrasting color. The contrast should have the same value as the first color. Cut four ½-in. by 18-in. (1.3-cm by 45-cm) strips of each; then tape them together in alternation.

Next select a different color from the original value gradation and incorporate it into a five-step polychromatic value and size gradation. Each strip in this section will have a different width. The widest strip will be 1¼ in. by 18 in. (3 cm by 45 cm); 1-in. (2.5-cm), ¾-in. (2-cm), 5/8-in. (1.5-cm), and 3/8-in. (1-cm) strips will follow. The light-to-dark gradation can proceed either from the widest to the narrowest strip or vice versa.

The final section is a simple light and dark contrast, and the two colors may be chosen from among those used in the completed sections. From each of these colors cut one 2-in. by 18-in. (5-cm by 45-cm) strip, and tape the two together.

You now have four strip sections, each measuring 4 in. by 18 in. (10 cm by 45 cm). Basing all your selections on the original value gradation helps to make the colors in the various sections more or less compatible.

Next, prepare a set or sets of templates that can be used together to form a 12-in. (31-cm) to 15-in. (38-cm) block pattern. You can use

Figure 5-12. Shapes were cut from the four different strip sections above to form the finished design.

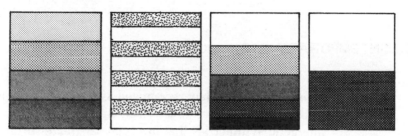

as many templates as you like, providing that each shape can be cut from the strip sections. The shapes can be planned to fit together to form a symmetrical image, or they can be arranged asymmetrically. Figure 5-12 shows a finished design and the four strip sections on which it was based.

An exercise such as this is intended to suggest the infinite variability of such a technique. In the process of puzzling over combinations of shapes and strip sections as well as color combinations, you will encounter a wealth of design problems that are better understood in such hands-on activity.

THE CONTEMPORARY STRIP QUILT

Nancy Crow is widely recognized as the leading exponent of the strip quilt. Her work is characterized by intense colors and dynamic and energetic symmetries that interplay to create surfaces of great sophistication and power.

Matisse Plain (Plate 16) employs a variety of single-width strip sections within a structure of nine concentric square modules. Rhomboids are cut from the strip sections and, after a triangle is attached at one end, become the sides of each square. A yellow-orange band outlines each of the nine modules, as well as the interior squares. The concentration of darker values at the outer sides of each module and lighter values at the center endows each unit with a sense of space-containing volume.

February Study 2 (Plate 20) is dominated by curved-seam elements and bold strip-pieced checkerboard borders that contain reversed value gradations in strip piecing. In addition, striped fabric is used in the central medallion area. The kaleidoscopic emergence of curved forms at the center of the quilt suggests a sense of energy being generated out from that center. The value gradations provide an interior light source that enhances the feeling of spatial depth in the quilt surface.

Black and white contrasts in strip piecing anchor the curved-seam forms to the surface of *March Study* (Plate 22). From behind the thick black lattice these curved forms appear, overlapping the center square area. Nancy depends on a rigid symmetry here to stabilize the juxtaposition of a large number of complex strip sections. The quilt breathes with a life of its own and reflects the unique aesthetic sensibilities of its maker.

The center focus is maintained in *Newe II* (Plate 21) as large curved forms move in from the sides of the surface and squeeze the narrow geometric forms into a confined space at the center of the quilt. Overlap again introduces a sense of space to the image. The kaleidoscopic fracturing of the surface provides an excitement that belies the symmetrical organization of the design. Here again Nancy's enthusiastic use of color saturates the surface with excitement. As jazz is to the history of music, so are these works to the history of quilt design.

In her strip-pieced quilts, Françoise Barnes creates an exotic world in which large geometric forms mirror each other with an almost primitive boldness. *Blue Metamorphosis* (Fig. 5-13 and Plate 19) is the liberation of a butterfly from its cocoon or the opening of an amaryllis—a mysterious dance of transformation. Blue and green shapes pull us into an unknown landscape behind the geometric figures on the surface of the quilt. The strip piecing is complemented by the use of

Figure 5-13. *Blue Metamorphosis* by Françoise Barnes. 1979. 75 in. by 75 in. (191 cm by 191 cm). Machine-pieced, hand-quilted cotton blends; polyester batting. Quilted by Bertha Mast. Photo courtesy of the artist.

Figure 5-14. *Black Metamorphosis* by Françoise Barnes. 1979. 73 in. by 73 in. (186 cm by 186 cm). Machine-pieced, hand-quilted cotton blends; polyester batting. Quilted by Mattie Raber. Photo courtesy of the artist.

Figure 5-15. Detail of *Black Metamorphosis* by Françoise Barnes.

printed stripes near the center and at the outer sides. Fragments of a printed palm tree diffuse the energetic rhythm and motion of the bargello-style print used in the center of the quilt.

The same surface composition is reinterpreted with a dark border in *Black Metamorphosis* (Figs. 5-14 and 5-15).

In *Escape* (Fig. 5-16) Françoise leads us to an abandoned hide-away to witness the passing of daylight as sunset purples and oranges move in from the edges of the pieced design. Here the fracturing of the surface space by the contrast of strip-pieced sections creates a flickering light that interacts with the oncoming darkness.

The vertical arrangement of forms in *Eyes of Isis* (Figs. 5-17 and 5-18) takes on a totemlike dignity and power. Strip piecing is used effectively to create the "cat's eyes," as well as the large blossoming

Figure 5-16. *Escape* by Françoise Barnes. 1979. 62 in. by 62 in. (158 cm by 158 cm). Machine pieced, hand-quilted cotton blends; polyester batting. Quilted by Louina Yoder. Photo courtesy of the artist.

forms at the center of the quilt. A well-integrated quilting design establishes diagonal movements in the surface that contrast with the rigid verticality of the design.

Although Radka Donnell-Vogt's quilt *Wholeness* (Plate 18) is not a strip-pieced quilt, her use of striped fabrics suggests the same crazing of the surface attainable with the strip technique as illustrated in Fig. 5-8. The symmetry established in the way the rectangular panels of fabric are ordered is contradicted by the freely colored dye samples that become cloudlike forms at the center of the quilt. The frenetic machine quilting is a subtle counterpoint to the overall restraint of the color surface.

Figure 5-17. *Eyes of Isis* by Françoise Barnes. 1978. 80 in. by 84 in. (203 cm by 213 cm). Machine-pieced, hand-quilted cotton blends; polyester batting. Quilted by an Amish woman.

Figure 5-18. Detail of *Eyes of Isis* by Francoise Barnes.

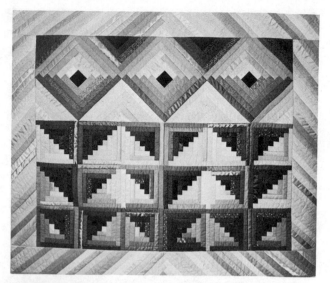

Log Cabin: New Ways With an Old Form

6

One of the things quiltmakers like most about the Log Cabin quilt is its variability. There is something appealing about a system of construction that remains unchanging and yet holds the potential for creating hundreds of different design surfaces.

Simply put, the technique of Log Cabin construction (also called *pressed piecing*) involves the sewing of strips of fabric around a small center shape. The result is a repeat unit that consists of two or more short-to-long gradations of fabric strips. The strips are sewn around the center shape in one of several sequences, depending on the desired image. As the strips are sewn, color contrasts and light and dark arrangements are assigned to different parts of the block.

While it is one of the primary attractions of the process, the look of the Log Cabin quilt can also be its major drawback, at least for anyone who wants to explore beyond the tradition. Although Log Cabin lends itself to endless original variation, it is a real challenge to the quiltmaker searching for innovation.

The Log Cabin repeat structure can be divided into two basic types. On the one hand are those blocks in which the strips are sewn in a clockwise or counterclockwise sequence around the center shape. On the other hand are blocks in which strips are sewn on opposite sides of the center shape. We will examine both types and their variations.

CLOCKWISE-SEQUENCE PATTERNS

The numerical sequence in Fig. 6-1 indicates the order in which each piece of fabric is sewn to form a clockwise pattern. The strips may also be attached in a counterclockwise progression. It matters less in what direction you proceed than that you are faithful to that direction.

The basic block pattern in this category is the square containing a square center. This is the structure generally used to support diagonal light-and-dark contrast arrangements. The number of steps out from the center is variable, as are the widths of the strips. These may be, for example, of the same width as the center square, or half as wide. They may also be wider than the center square, as shown in Fig. 6-2.

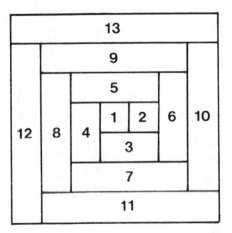

Figure 6-1. Clockwise sequence pattern.

The center square may be turned 45 degrees so that it is set at a diagonal to the outside block. In this arrangement some strips eventually run off into the corners without joining any other strips in the block (see Fig. 6-5).

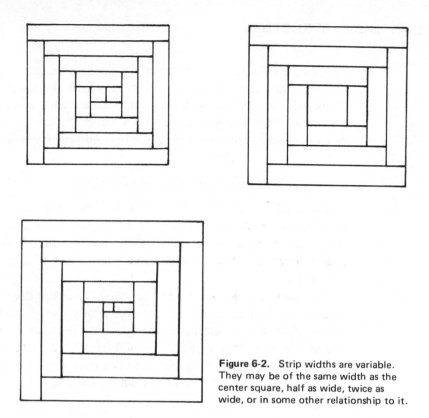

Figure 6-2. Strip widths are variable. They may be of the same width as the center square, half as wide, twice as wide, or in some other relationship to it.

Different widths can be used simultaneously. They may grade from wide to narrow, or from narrow to wide, as in Fig. 6-3. They may be arranged on opposite sides of the diagonal, thus forming off-center Log Cabin blocks, as in Fig. 6-4.

The corner square Log Cabin block shown in Fig. 6-5 is technically a clockwise-sequence pattern. The progression from one side to the

Figure 6-3. Width gradations in the clockwise-sequence block.

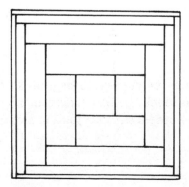
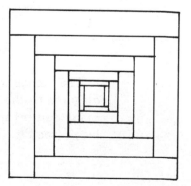

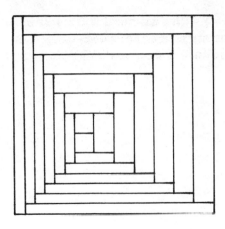

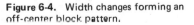

Figure 6-4. Width changes forming an off-center block pattern.

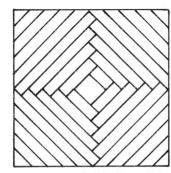

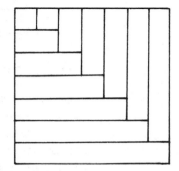

Figure 6-5. Diagonal center square and corner square patterns.

next is simply repeated over and over, with gradually longer strips of fabric.

Shapes other than the square can be used at the centers of these patterns. They will change not only the finished shape of the strips but also the shape of the block itself. The triangular center (Fig. 6-6) will produce a triangular repeat, and the strips will no longer finish as

Figure 6-6. Triangular and diamond center patterns.

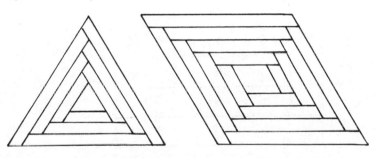

rectangles but as trapezoids. Beginning with a diamond will result in a diamond-shaped repeat in which the strips are rhomboids of increasing size. A hexagonal center will produce a six-sided block made up of trapezoidal strips as in Fig. 6-7.

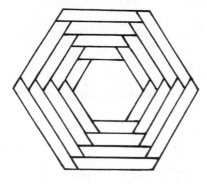

Figure 6-7. Hexagonal Log Cabin pattern.

OPPOSITE-SIDE SEQUENCES

In these patterns strips are sewn on opposite sides of the center shape. Figure 6-8 shows a simple block unit, indicating the numerical sequence in which strips are attached. Normally, two strips of a single size are attached one after the other on opposite sides. The next two strips show a proportional increase based on the first two that were attached. These patterns are historically called *Courthouse Steps* blocks.

Square center blocks can contain strips each the same width as the center. The number of strips in the sequence is variable. Strip widths can also be varied. They can grade from narrow at the center to wider at the outside, or vice versa, as in Fig. 6-9.

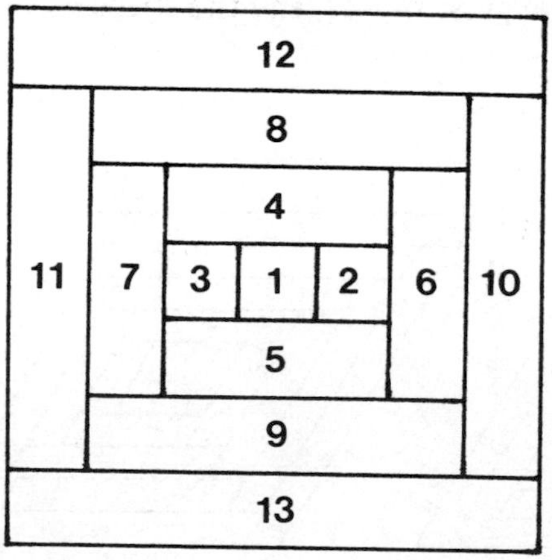

Figure 6-8. Opposite-sequence pattern.

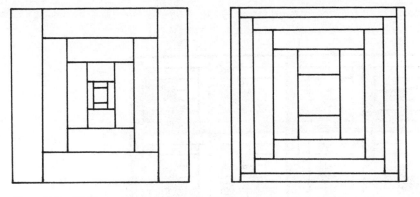

Figure 6-9. Width gradations in the opposite-sequence block.

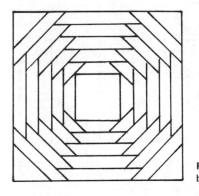

Figure 6-10. Pineapple Log Cabin block.

The Pineapple Log Cabin block (Fig. 6-10) is a popular unit based on an opposite-side sequence. Strips of equal size are first attached to each of the four sides of the center square. The next four are attached at 45 degree angles to the corners of the center square. The next four are again set parallel to the center square, and so on. Eventually the strips stop meeting and move out to the corners.

Clockwise-sequence blocks appear to offer a wider design range in terms of structure than do opposite-sequence patterns. Both types, however, depend on light and dark contrasts and color and fabric interactions to become exciting design surfaces.

LIGHT AND DARK AND THE LOG CABIN QUILT

The Log Cabin block as well as the repeat-block surface are based on light and dark contrasts. All the traditional Log Cabin variations, among them Straight Furrow, Barn Raising, Courthouse Steps, and Sunshine and Shadow, depend on these contrasts for their particular surface arrangement.

111

Figure 6-11. Diagonal light and dark variations.

113 Figure 6-12. Diagonal light and dark variations.

In square-center clockwise-sequence patterns, lights and darks have been traditionally distributed on opposite sides of the diagonal formed by the butting of the fabric strips. This basically divides the block into two triangular areas, one light and one dark. By arranging identical blocks any number of variations can be created. Some examples are shown in Figs. 6-11 and 6-12.

There are actually four triangular divisions in these clockwise-sequence blocks. The lights and darks can also be arranged to emphasize these, as in Fig. 6-13.

Figure 6-13. Lights and darks arranged to emphasize triangular subdivisions.

Figure 6-14. Log Cabin sampler by the author, 1978. 30 in. by 30 in. (76 cm by 76 cm). Cotton; machine Log Cabin technique II.

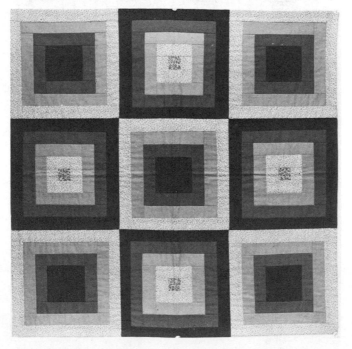

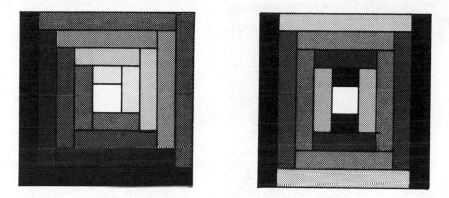

Figure 6-15. Value gradations applied to size gradations in the Log Cabin strip sequences.

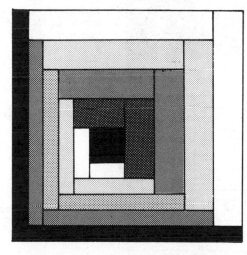

Figure 6-16. Value gradation in the off-center Log Cabin block.

The image of concentric squares floating as planes in the two-dimensional surface can be produced with light and dark contrasts as gradation. In Fig. 6-14, each block is made up of sets of four strips of each of four values of green fabric. They suggest a visual push-and-pull effect. This arrangement could be duplicated in the opposite-sequence block.

The size gradations in the strip sequence suggest light and dark contrasts carried out as value gradations. This can be worked on opposite sides of the diagonal or worked out from each of the four sides of the center square, as in Fig. 6-15.

The off-center Log Cabin block is especially receptive to light and dark contrasts as seen in value gradations (Fig. 6-16). The contrast

Figure 6-17. Log Cabin variation sampler by Maria McCormick-Snyder. Copyright 1978. 20 in. by 20 in. (51 cm by 51 cm). Cotton; machine Log Cabin technique I. Collection of the author.

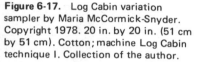

Figure 6-18. Courthouse Steps blocks in traditional arrangement.

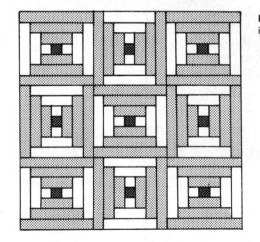

of the two strip widths creates a curve along one diagonal, and light and dark contrasts along this curve can help to heighten spatial illusions in the quilt surface. Maria McCormick-Snyder used these contrasts effectively in the off-center sampler in Fig. 6-17.

The traditional Courthouse Steps variation is said to represent a pedimented Greek Revival courthouse, with white columns flanking a doorway where the judge in black robes stands (see Fig. 6-18). This

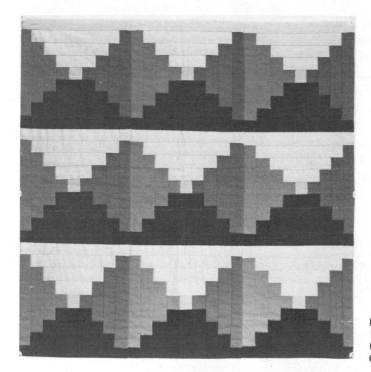

Figure 6-19. Opposite sequence sampler by the author. 1978. 20 in. by 20 in. (51 cm by 51 cm). Cotton; machine Log Cabin technique II.

Figure 6-20. Width gradation in an opposite-sequence pattern.

romantic notion is surely afterthought. The opposite-sequence block is pure abstraction.

Graded light and dark contrasts can be used to create light and spatial effects in the opposite-sequence block. A four-sided pyramid is suggested in Figs. 6-19 and 3-9. When combined with a size gradation, these contrasts can create fascinating light effects. As strips get narrower (see Fig. 6-20), contrasts are softened and diffused. If they get narrow enough, our eyes will begin to blend adjoining colors and those areas will seem fuzzy or out of focus.

Value gradations were used in the Pineapple Log Cabin sampler shown in Fig. 6-21 and Plate 36.

Figure 6-21. Pineapple Log Cabin sampler by the author. 1977. 24 in. by 24 in. (61 cm by 61 cm). Cotton; hand-pieced.

COLOR DISCOVERIES WITH LOG CABIN

Because the geometric structure of the Log Cabin block is so simple, the form lends itself to color experiments and explorations. I have used it in just this way in numerous color workshops. Much of what we discussed in Chapter 3 can be applied to the Log Cabin structure with interesting results.

Color exercises in Log Cabin can be worked out in colored paper. Cut strips of color on the length of the sheet, in either ¼-in. (6-mm) or ½-in. (1.3-cm) widths. You won't have to think about seam allowances when working in paper. A paper glue will be needed to fix your strips to a blank sheet of white paper.

VALUE CHANGE

A color value change can be effected in the first exercise. Select two colors you like together, and then choose three more values of each of those. You will now have two monochromatic value gradations. Cut one or two strips of each color.

On the blank sheet, draw two ½-in. (1.3-cm) squares several inches (or about 9 cm) apart. These will be the centers of the two blocks. The colors for these centers will be chosen after the rest of the strips are glued.

Construct a clockwise sequence pattern in four steps around the first blank square. Use one of the value gradations in one diagonal half of the block. The other will be used in the second diagonal half. Begin with the lightest values of each of the colors, and proceed outward to the darkest, as in Fig. 6-15. Around the second blank center square arrange the same monochromatic gradations, but begin with the darkest values and work outward to the lightest.

When the strip arrangements are completed, begin your selection of a center color for the two blocks. This should be a new color and not one used in the outer arrangements. You will want to change the apparent value of that color by placing it in each of the blank center spaces. Try a number of different colors until you find one that you feel effects the change most dramatically.

This value change was worked out in the cut-paper samples shown in Plate 35.

INTENSITY CHANGE

A similar exercise can be carried out with color intensity. As you recall, intensity is the strength of a color—its visual impact relative to the colors around it. This investigation will demonstrate that intensity is not so much a property of the color itself as a variable characteristic influenced by surrounding colors.

First choose a color you like that seems to be intense. Cut two ½-in. (1.3-cm) squares and glue them a few inches apart on a blank sheet of paper. You will complete the first block before considering the second and the desired intensity change.

Select two new colors that you will use in a three-step opposite-sequence arrangement. These two colors should have about the same value and should look well together and with the center square. Cut several strips of each and glue them in place around the first center square.

Next choose two different colors for the second block. In making the selection you must decide whether you want to make the center square more intense than it appears in the first block or less intense. The colors you choose should have about the same value as the colors in the first block. If not, you will probably also effect a value change, and this would make the intensity change harder to perceive. You will probably need to try several combinations before arriving at a satisfactory solution.

An intensity change is demonstrated in the opposite-sequence cut-paper samples in Plate 35. The subtractive function of color was used to decrease the intensity of the pink center on the predominantly red ground, while a temperature contrast was used in the other block to intensify that light red center.

POLYCHROMATIC VALUE GRADATION

The off-center clockwise-sequence block in six steps shown in Fig. 6-4 provides an excellent foundation for the following exercise.

Choose two distinct polychromatic value gradations. The first will be a six-step gradation in a cool color range. Try to select six distinct cool colors, as well as six distinct and consecutive values. As discussed in Chapter 3, the polychromatic gradation should follow the natural color order. Your second set of six colors will be chosen in a warm color range, and also in a light to dark gradation.

Cut one of the sets into strips each ½-in. (1.3-cm) wide. Cut the other into ¼-in. (6-mm) strips. You will need two strips of each color to complete the exercise.

Mark on a white sheet the blank center square, and begin arranging the strips, using the warm polychromatic gradation on one half of the diagonal of the block and the cool gradation on the other. You may begin with the lightest values in each set and work outward to dark, or vice versa. When you have completed the arrangement, select a color for the center square and glue it in place.

The Log Cabin sampler by Maria McCormick-Snyder shown in Fig. 6-17 is made up of four off-center blocks based on two polychromatic value gradations. The cool set of colors is used in the narrow strips, and the warm colors are used in the wider strips. In the cool set the value gradation proceeds from dark at the center to light at the outside of the block. In the warm set the progression is from light to dark at the outside.

I encourage you to explore color interactions with the Log Cabin block. It is a convenient device for this type of work, and clearly demonstrates the creative mileage that can yet be had from this ancient design structure.

CONTEMPORARY LOG CABIN TECHNIQUES

Although it has been traditionally executed by hand, the Log Cabin technique is well suited to machine sewing. In general Log Cabin machine sewing is easier than the traditional pressed piecing technique that uses a block-size foundation square. It is stronger and gives a crisper, more precise seam line than does the hand technique. Above all it is quicker, providing a finished product in far less time than would be required by hand.

I will present two methods for machine Log Cabin. The first is carried out without a foundation, resulting in a quilt top only. The second uses the foundation square and incorporates quilt batting, accomplishing both the piecing and the quilting in one step.

MACHINE LOG CABIN I

Those of you who prefer to piece a top only and then quilt in the conventional way will find this method ideal. For maximum speed and efficiency, however, it is necessary that you prepare the strips accurately and organize your work space. Your machine should be in good working order and you should have a small ironing board and an iron alongside the machine so that you can press without getting up.

Strips of fabric for Log Cabin are marked and cut as for strip piecing. Each strip must include seam allowance. If you plan the strips to finish 1-in. (2.5-cm) wide in the design, you must cut them 1½-in. (3.8-cm) wide. If they are to finish 3 in. (7.5 cm), cut them 3½-in. (9-cm) wide.

Mark the strip lengths parallel to the selvage for least amount of stretch, as in Fig. 5-1. If you need to mark on the crosswise grain, be sure to handle the fabric strips with more care as you sew them together.

You can measure down from the selvage to mark off the cutting lines, or you can use templates for the various widths (including seam allowance) that you need to cut. (See the description of marking strips in Chapter 5.) Each piece in the block will be cut from these long strips as needed.

To begin the sewing you will need to cut the center shape, either by using a ruler to measure and mark it on one of the strips or by using a template. If this first shape is not precise, it will help to throw off the rest of the block.

Take the first color you'll attach and place that strip right side to the center shape. Pin them together. Sew the two pieces together, taking a ¼-in. (6-mm) seam allowance. You will not need to back-tack until you get to the outsides of the block, as each seam end will be crossed over by another. After the seam is sewn, cut off the strip length in excess of the center shape as in Fig. 6-22. Press the two sewn shapes, seams open or to one side as you prefer.

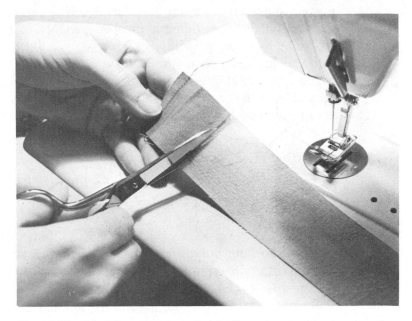

Figure 6-22. After the center square and the first strip color are sewn, the strip is cut to the size of the center.

You are now ready for the second strip color. Lay this strip right side to the first two pieces and sew another ¼-in. (6-mm) seam allowance. Cut off the excess as shown in Fig. 6-23 and then press. Proceed in this way, either sewing in a clockwise or counterclockwise sequence or sewing on opposite sides of the center shape.

Completed blocks are attached to one another in the conventional way, care being taken that corners meet accurately.

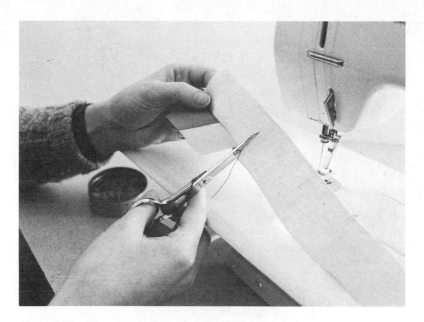

Figure 6-23. The second strip color is attached and then cut to match the combined length of the center square and the first strip color.

It's important to be aware that any slight deviation from a straight ¼-in. (6-mm) seam in sewing the strips together will be revealed when you get to the outside of the block. It may not be precisely square, or triangular, or whatever shape it's supposed to be. In most cases, very slight irregularities won't be amplified enough to be really noticeable. However, it's best to watch for this as you join the strips, and to make adjustments before you get to the outside.

MACHINE LOG CABIN II

Because I do most of my own pieced work and quilting by hand, I appreciate an occasional change in the form of a fast, one-step approach. This machine Log Cabin variation allows me to piece and quilt simultaneously, with only a minimum of hand work in the finishing.

Strips of fabric are prepared as described above. If the presser foot on your machine cannot be used as a ¼-in. (6-mm) seam gauge, you will need to mark the sewing line on each strip, in addition to marking the cutting line. You can do this by measuring a line parallel to and ¼ in. (6 mm) from each cutting line you mark. If you are using templates to mark the strip widths, you can likewise prepare templates ¼-in. (6-mm) narrower to mark the sewing line on each strip, as in Fig. 6-24.

123

Figure 6-24. Here the sewing line is marked on a 1½-in. (3.8-cm) strip by using a ruler that is 1¼-in. (3.2-cm) wide.

You cannot use the seam gauge etched into the needle plate when sewing these blocks. The fabric foundation and the batting onto which you sew the strips cover this plate completely.

The foundation can be a solid or printed fabric. I have used both and prefer a busy, small-scale print on the back. This disguises the construction and the back looks like one solid piece of fabric when finished. You may prefer to emphasize and display the construction by using solid-color fabric as the foundation.

The foundation is cut ¼ in. (6 mm) larger all around than the desired finish size. If you are planning a finished block that is 10-in. (25.4-cm) square, the foundation will begin as a 10½-in. (26.7-cm) square. Cut a template for marking the foundations.

You can omit batting if you prefer a flatter, lighter-weight piece. Batting, however, gives a softness to the geometric forms in the Log Cabin design. It also helps to create the low-relief effect that hand or machine quilting provides in a conventional quilt.

A thin polyester batting is preferable to a thick one for several reasons. Thick battings tend to get caught on the presser foot when you are moving the work under and out from the needle area. A thick batting will also absorb into its heft a greater percentage of each fabric strip as it is sewn. This can result in a significant reduction in the size of the top strip area, as well as in the size of the whole block.

I have used polyester fleece interlining and find that its characteristics lend itself to machine Log Cabin. It is thin and dense, and similar in texture to felt. It is cut and handled very much like fabric, unlike regular quilt battings. Since it has more body than most quilt battings, it does not drape as softly on a bed but lends itself well to wall pieces.

You should prepare a template for marking the batting. The batting is cut to the finished size of the block, or just slightly smaller. When the batting has been cut, center it on the foundation square and pin it in place. Mark off the center of the block on the batting by ruling crossing lines from opposite corners, as in Fig. 6-25.

Cut the center square and pin it in place, being careful that it is aligned parallel with the outsides of the block (Fig. 6-26). The center square should be ¼ in. (6 mm) larger all around than its finished size.

Figure 6-25. Templates for foundation and batting, with batting square pinned to a foundation. The center of the block is located by ruling diagonal lines from corner to corner.

Figure 6-26. Center square pinned in place on batting and foundation

The second piece to be attached has the same length as the center square. Lay a strip of fabric next to the center, and cut a corresponding length in the new color. (You may prefer to sew the strip color in place first, and then cut it, as in Fig. 6-27.) Pin it right side to the first piece, and sew through all layers, using the presser foot or a sewing line as the seam gauge.

You can back-tack at the beginning and end of each seam. This won't show on the back if the backing fabric is a small, busy print, and the bobbin thread matches that print. Be sure to cut off thread ends close to the work.

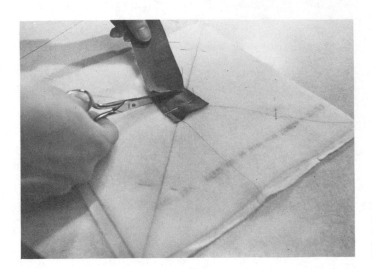

Figure 6-27. The first strip color is sewn right side to the center square, and then cut the same length as the center. You may prefer to cut before stitching.

Figure 6-28. The bobbin thread is drawn up from the back by gently lifting it with the top needle thread. Once a loop is brought up, it can be drawn through with a needle.

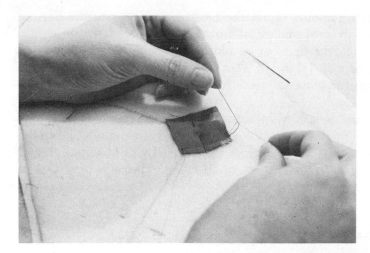

Figure 6-29. The two thread ends are knotted to secure the stitching.

I prefer to draw the bobbin thread up through the top and tie off on the inside of the work. In this way there are no indications of back-tacking on the back of the work. Figures 6-28 and 6-29 show how this is done.

As each strip is sewn, remove the pins and finger-press the strip back onto the batting. Pin it in place, as shown in Fig. 6-30. As you sew in sequence out from the center, you will use the attached strips to indicate the size of each new strip you cut. When the strips are all

Figure 6-30. The sewn strips indicate the length of each new strip in the sequence. Here the strip is cut before being sewn.

attached, the top should equal the backing in size, and the batting should be ¼ in. (6 mm) smaller all around.

To join two blocks first cut an additional strip of the backing fabric. This can be cut 1¼-in. (3.2-cm) or 1½-in. (3.8-cm) wide. This strip will be used to close the seam formed when two blocks are sewn together.

Place the two blocks right sides together, carefully aligning the outside edges. Pin along the side where they will be joined. Place the extra strip along the sewing edge, right side to the backing fabric, as shown in Fig. 6-31. Sew through all layers, taking a ¼-in. (6-mm) seam allowance.

Figure 6-31. Two blocks are pinned right sides together. Closure strip is sewn along seam as blocks are joined.

When the pins are removed, the seam allowance can be trimmed evenly. The extra strip attached to the back of the blocks is now used to enclose the seam. Lay the blocks flat on your work surface, backing side up. Fold the strip over the seam, as in Fig. 6-32. Pin it in place, and stitch it down to the backing with a blind or an overcast stitch.

This method is also used to join two rows of blocks. To avoid too much thickness at points where the corners of blocks join, plan the closures to go in one direction in one row and in the opposite direction in the other, as in Fig. 6-33.

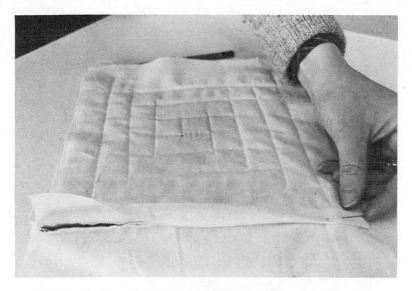

Figure 6-32. Binding strip is folded over seams, pinned in place, and hand-stitched to the backing.

Figure 6-33. Binding closures are turned to the right in one row and to the left in the other, in order to minimize bulk at the joints.

CONTEMPORARY LOG CABIN QUILTS

I used the technique described above to make the quilt *Poppies* (Figs. 6-34 and 6-35 and Plate 13). Two different block sizes were used in addition to the triangular units that complete the large rectangular area in which the blossoms open. I found that the use of the different

129

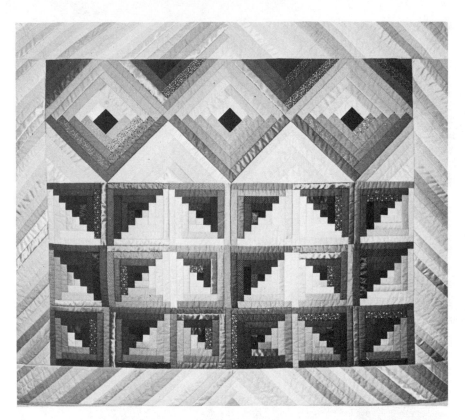

Figure 6-34. *Poppies* by the author. 1979. 56 in. by 65 in. (142 cm by 165 cm). Machine Log Cabin technique II. Cotton, satin, velveteen; Pellon fleece batting. Collection of I.B.M. Corp.

Figure 6-35. Detail of *Poppies* by the author.

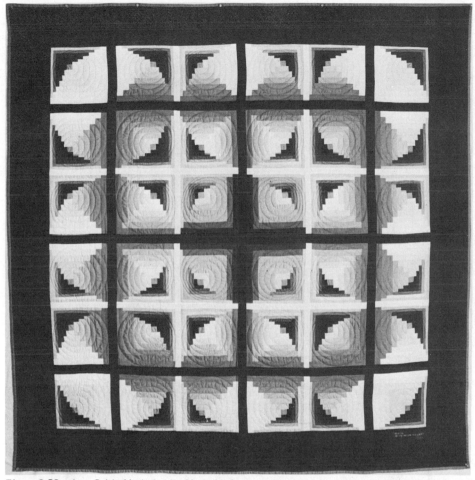

Figure 6-36. *Log Cabin Variation* by Maria McCormick-Snyder. Copyright 1978. 73 in. by 73 in. (186 cm by 186 cm). Cotton; polyester batting. Machine Log Cabin technique I; hand-quilted. Photo courtesy of the artist.

fabrics against the fleece batting in the machine technique made it more difficult to achieve the precision necessary to make each block uniform. When it came time to join the blocks, I had to push and pull and adjust to achieve the degree of accuracy I wanted. The completed image suggests the types of geometric flower forms found in cross-stitch embroidery as well as in knitted designs.

The off-center Log Cabin block was used by Maria McCormick-Snyder in her *Log Cabin Variation*, shown in Figs. 6-36 and 6-37 and in Plate 17. The repeat blocks contain both monochromatic and polychromatic value gradations. The directions of the gradations within each block are reversed, so that a light and dark contrast is created. These contrasts result in circular forms which appear on the surface.

131

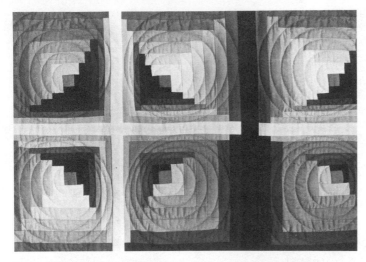

Figure 6-37. Detail of *Log Cabin Variation* by Maria McCormick-Snyder. Photo courtesy of the artist.

Figure 6-38. *Art Deco* by Maria McCormick-Snyder. Copyright 1979. 84 in. by 84 in. (213 cm by 213 cm). Cotton, satin, velvet; polyester batting. Machine Log Cabin technique I; hand-quilted. Photo courtesy of the artist.

Figure 6-39. Detail of *Art Deco* by Maria McCormick-Snyder. Photo courtesy of the artist.

The blocks are set together with black and white lattice strips, and these form horizontal and vertical grids that intersect these circles. The quilting design in graduated concentric circles gives a fluidity to the surface pattern that complements the smooth blending of colors.

This quilt was sewn by using Machine Log Cabin technique I. With the top completed, the quilting of the three layers was done at a quilt frame.

The reference to an open window in Maria's quilt *Art Deco* (Figs. 6-38 and 6-39) is appropriate because the quilt is, in fact, a breath of fresh air giving a completely new look to an old form. The quilt combines both Log Cabin construction and conventional pieced work to create the curves that move across the surface. There are no curved seams, however. The variegated strips are pieced of shorter lengths cut at slight diagonals. These diagonals are then matched to create the curved seams. The use of the satins, velvets, and corduroys in addition to cotton broadcloth creates a richly textured surface to which the viewer can't help but be attracted.

Bē Smith has used both clockwise-sequence and opposite-sequence blocks to depict an early morning landscape in *Tennessee Sunrise* (Fig. 6-40). Country ginghams and calicoes underscore the rural nature of the scene, in which the sun rises over hills and valleys.

In *Storm Over Alexandria* (Fig. 6-41) the artist has used an abstract geometric composition of clockwise-sequence blocks to suggest the mass of a large thunderhead. Light and dark contrasts define the jagged lightning bolts, and the reflection of these zigzag diagonals in lighter value arrangements suggests the reverberation of thunder and the slow movement of the storm cloud.

Figure 6-40. *Tennessee Sunrise* by Bē Smith. 1976. 70 in. by 70 in. (178 cm by 178 cm); cotton. Machine Log Cabin. Photo courtesy of the artist.

Figure 6-41. *Storm Over Alexandria* by Bē Smith. 1978. 84 in. by 120 in. (213 cm by 305 cm). Machine Log Cabin. Cotton, silk; polyester fiberfill. Photo courtesy of the artist.

Quilting: Line and Texture In the Quilt Surface

In quilting we encounter the essence of the quilt, both as art form and as craft. The stitching that travels through and secures the layers of the textile sandwich defines the nature of the quilt. The object can be any size, shape, or color. It can be functional or nonfunctional, whole-cloth, pieced, appliquéd, embroidered, painted, printed, or a combination of any or all of these, and possibly more. If it is quilted, it is a quilt.

As I sit here putting thoughts about quilting on paper, I experience an impulse to leave the typewriter and pick up where I left the quilting on a work in progress. For me, quilting holds a strong attraction, though I'm not sure I fully understand why.

I know that the texture it gives to the surface of a quilt and the tactile appeal that results is part of it. The interplay of closely quilted areas with open areas as well as the interplay of the quilted design with the pieced, appliqué, or other surface design can provide pleasing visual texture. Light and shadow enter very much into this. A soft, diffused light will diminish that texture and subordinate the quilting design to any other surface design that might be part of the quilt. A strong sidelight will carve the design more boldly into the quilt. In all quilts, but especially in the whole-cloth quilt, this delineation can suggest the actual carving of a low-relief surface. In fact, this is exactly what it is.

Another reason I may be drawn to quilting is the singular importance of every stitch. To a degree, this importance is a contradiction. Each single stitch, if isolated, has no importance. It is a stitch and nothing else. Taken collectively, however, the stitches in the quilt define the linear design, both as a surface pattern and as sculpture. Each stitch is as important as every other. Each is created by the same action of the hand or the machine. Each is ultimately subordinate to the whole.

The act of quilting by itself is pure technique. In the context of the design of the quilt as a whole, however, it becomes the conduit for the expression of creative ideas. Although it's not by nature a creative act, in the design of the quilt it becomes a manifestation of that act.

I have amazed myself at times by hand-quilting for upwards of twelve hours a day, sometimes for days on end, to finish a piece. At those times the quilting often became a tedious and tiring involvement. Sometimes my body ached, and sometimes my mind ached. Although I could enjoy the rhythm of the process and the making of each single stitch, at times I would have appreciated doing anything else. Always, though, I could look ahead to the finished product, and watch it materialize.

THE WHOLE-CLOTH QUILT

NOTES ON MATERIALS AND TECHNIQUE

The whole-cloth quilt is a textile sandwich in which the top layer, the surface on which the visual image is expressed, is a solid-color fabric. Historically whole-cloth has also included printed and painted fabric surfaces that were whole lengths of yardage. Quilts made of these figured surfaces were whole-cloth quilts. My concern here is with solid-color whole-cloth quilts.

In choosing materials for a whole-cloth quilt, it's important to consider the nature of the quilting technique and its intended purpose.

In hand quilting, needle and thread are guided through the layers in what we call a running stitch. The needle is held almost parallel to the surface of the quilt. The needle exits completely from the top side of the work, but not from the back. When part of the needle goes through the back layer, part of it is still exposed on the top. Between each visible stitch on front and back is a space.

In machine quilting, the needle operates perpendicularly to the quilt surface, moving mechanically up and down. The top needle thread is guided through the layers of the quilt to interlock with the bobbin thread below. The stitches line up end to end, with no spaces between them.

Both hand and machine quilting serve the same purpose. They delineate a surface design and help create a physical texture.

Because of the nature of the hand running stitch, there are more restrictions on the types of fabrics that can be used satisfactorily. You must be able to guide the needle and thread in and out of the fabric with the least effort possible. Any fabric that is too thick or heavy or tightly woven to allow you to achieve a quick and even rhythm will make a normally time-consuming process many times longer. On the other hand, any fabric that is too loosely woven may not be strong enough to withstand the pressure of being tightly stretched and then quilted.

For hand stitching, most broadcloth-weight fabrics are suitable. Polished or glazed cotton or polished cotton and synthetic blends lend themselves to whole-cloth work because they catch light and emphasize the contrasts of hill and valley created by the quilting. Satin-weave fabrics may be used, but you may need to adjust the size of your quilting stitches so they aren't lost in the weave. The same holds true for fabrics such as velveteen, velvet, and corduroy. With these, small stitches may disappear into the nap of the fabric, with a consequent loss of linear definition in the surface design.

Because of the up-and-down motion of the machine stitch, you can use a wider range of fabrics. What is impractical for hand stitching may not be for machine.

Likewise, batting type and thickness will have a greater effect on hand than on machine stitching. The size of the spaces between the hand-quilted stitches is determined by the combined thickness of the top and backing fabrics and the batting. The thinner each layer is, the smaller the space between two stitches will be. If the spaces are small, the definition of the indented line will be sharpened, and so will the overall design.

Today, most quiltmakers use synthetic battings. These range in thickness from about ¼ in. (6 mm) to about 2 in. (5 cm). It's my experience that anything thicker than about ¾ in. (1.9 cm) is impractical for hand quilting.

Thicker battings may be sewn at the machine. However, you should be aware in planning a piece for machine quilting that the quilting will absorb some of the fabric, most noticeably if the batting is relatively thick.

Your choice of batting type and thickness will depend on your preferences. Each has characteristics that will produce a different look in the final result.

DESIGN FOR WHOLE-CLOTH: THE LINEAR ELEMENT

In the sense that whole-cloth quilt design originates with line, we can consider it a form of drawing. Lines move across the surface of the quilt. They may be straight lines or curved, short or long, intersecting or parallel. They may be broken lines, as with hand quilting, or they may be the unbroken lines of machine quilting.

The primary activity of lines in the whole-cloth quilt is to define shapes. Those shapes may be geometric or they may be organic. They

Figure 7-1. All-white stuffed quilt made by Helen Powell in Stamford, N.Y., about 1875. 84 in. by 84 in. (213 cm by 213 cm). Cotton; cotton batting. Collection of Marian Fraze.

may be nonrepresentational, or they may depict familiar forms. They may be arranged symmetrically or asymmetrically.

Line as Filler Pattern

Historically, sets of parallel lines and grids of intersecting lines were used to fill background space in the whole-cloth quilt. These filler patterns were usually used to flatten the fabric area around representational images as well as around abstract geometric forms. The quilt shown in Fig. 7-1 displays the use of parallel lines to give added definition to the stuffed plant forms.

Filler patterns can be evenly spaced sets of parallel lines or grids made up of intersecting horizontal and vertical lines. They can be varied by changing straight lines to curved, by changing the directions of the lines, and by changing the relative proportions of the resulting modules (see Fig. 7-2).

By curving them, sets of parallel lines can be made to take on a fluid quality as they undulate across the quilt surface. Grading the

Figure 7-2. Grid variations for filler patterns.

size of the intervals between the lines can increase the sense of progression and movement. Line can be suggested by splitting and shifting actual lines so that the eye perceives line that is not actually there, as in Fig. 7-3.

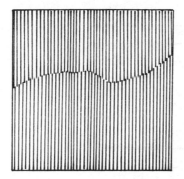

Figure 7-3. Line is suggested by splitting and shifting the set of parallel lines.

Grid fillers can be regularly spaced horizontal and vertical lines perpendicular to each other (the basic graph-paper grid), or the lines may meet at angles other than 90 degrees. The intervals between the lines may be graded, so that the effect of plaid fabric is seen. The modules created in the grid may be consistent throughout, or they may grade in size from small to large. The grid lines may remain parallel throughout, or they may change position so that if extended they would eventually cross adjoining lines.

Line as Repeat Figure

Apart from any naturalistic or representational form that you might draw and use as a figure in a whole-cloth surface, there are unlimited geometric nonfigurative images that can be used to create pattern.

Patterns of radiating lines may be contained in whole or in part within the boundaries of a repeat module (Fig. 7-4). Radiating lines share a common point of origin. The lines may be spaced at regular intervals, or they may be arranged irregularly. Within the module, the point of radiation may be at the center of the unit or may be placed off-center.

Lines may form concentric figures within the module (Fig. 7-5). These may share a common center, or the centers may be shifted to vary the interval spaces. (See Maria McCormick-Snyder's use of this shifting in her quilting pattern for the Log Cabin quilt in Fig. 6-37.)

Figure 7-4. Linear radiation patterns for use as repeat figures.

Figure 7-5. Concentric figures as repeat pattern units.

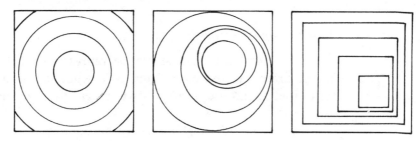

DESIGN FOR WHOLE-CLOTH: THE TEXTURAL ELEMENT

In addition to defining shapes and figures in the whole-cloth surface, you can create texture with line. The indentations formed by a single line of hand quilting create a visual as well as a tactile texture. Multiplied many times in a series of parallel lines or in grid form, these lines form highly textured areas.

Textured shapes will flatten out on the whole-cloth surface, leaving unquilted areas to rise in higher relief. These contrasts create interchanges of positive and negative forms. The quilted area may be perceived as the positive form, or vice versa. (See Fig. 7-23 for a perfect illustration of this interchange.)

The closer the quilting, the more highly textured that area will be. The texture is created not only by the linear development of the area, but also by the puckering of the fabric as stitches are taken through the three layers.

The contrast of closely quilted areas with more open areas can be used to suggest the effect of stuffing to achieve raised forms.

A NOTE ON STUFFED WORK

In the past the stuffing of quilted forms with extra batting was done on all types of quilts, but most frequently on whole-cloth surfaces. In large part this had to do with the fact that thin natural-fiber battings lost their loft over a period of time, and the designs flattened out. With stuffing this didn't happen. Stuffing gave a richness to the surface, and that was also a consideration.

Figures 7-6, 7-7, and 7-8 illustrate the traditional stuffing technique. Small holes are made in the quilted shapes with the end of a blunt-ended needle or other narrow tool. This is done on the side of the quilt that has the more loosely woven fabric. A narrow strand of batting is carefully guided into the middle layer. When the area is filled, the hole is closed by pushing the threads of the weave back together with the needle.

Figures 7-9 and 7-10 show the front and back of a stuffed Pineapple design in the quilt shown in Fig. 7-1. Notice that small wisps of cotton protrude from the stuffing holes, indicating that the threads were not completely returned to their original positions.

Figure 7-6. A small hole is made with an improvised plastic bodkin in the linen surface of this quilted sampler.

Figure 7-7. A strand of cotton batting is gently guided into the quilted space.

Figure 7-8. The hole is closed by poking the threads of the fabric back in place.

Figure 7-9. Front detail of stuffed figure from quilt shown in Fig. 7-1.

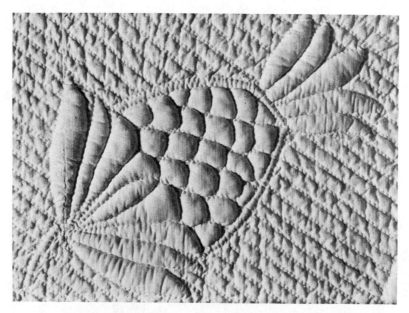

144

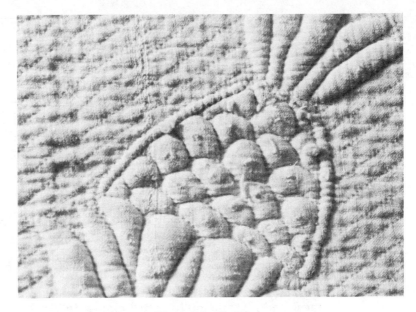

Figure 7-10. Back detail of Pineapple in Fig. 7-9.

A PROJECT IN WHOLE-CLOTH

Work out on paper a series of linear filler patterns and modular repeat patterns. Keep in mind as you do these that the lines represent indentations in the surface of the quilt, and will create visual as well as actual textures.

I suggest an approximate size for this project of 45-in. (114.3-cm) square. This takes into account the standard width of most fabrics. This size is arbitrary, however, and you can make a larger project if you wish.

If you piece together two widths of a fabric to make a larger whole, try to incorporate the seam line into the stitched design. In the quilt in Fig. 7-28, I joined a 10-in. (25.4-cm) width to a 50-in. (127-cm) width to make a 60-in. (152-cm) quilt. The seam line is actually the bottommost horizontal grid line in the design. A line of quilting was done just alongside the seam.

Figure 7-11 shows several diagrams indicating ways in which the quilt surface can be organized. Each is made up of a modular structure. One is enclosed by two borders, the other by one. The third structure does not incorporate a border. You may work within one of these grid structures, or work out your own surface organization.

Transfer the grid structure directly to the top fabric with ruler

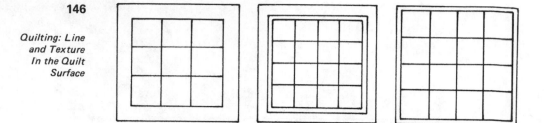

Figure 7-11. Diagrams for modular composition of a whole-cloth project.

and pencil. This is most easily done by first pressing the fabric across the middle from top to bottom and then from side to side. From these creases you can then measure out to the desired dimensions, marking off subdivisions as you proceed.

I have discussed techniques for marking designs on fabric, as well as hand- and machine-quilting techniques, in *The Quiltmaker's Handbook* (Prentice-Hall, 1978). If you are using white or another light-colored fabric, it is possible that you will be able to trace through your fabric. This would allow you to work out your design full-size on paper. You can transfer your image directly to fabric with pencil. You can also use dressmaker's carbon and a tracing wheel to mark the quilting design. A light or dark pounce through a perforated paper pattern works quickly and accurately.

I used perforated patterns to transfer the repeat images to the surface of *Suntreader/Monophony* (Figs. 7-28 and 7-29). The linear units were first drawn with compass on heavyweight tracing paper. The perforation was done on an unthreaded sewing machine by turning the wheel manually at the biggest stitch setting. I then used cinnamon to transfer the image to the fabric. This pounce was used with the quilt stretched taut in the hoop, one area at a time. The overall grid had been drawn on the fabric with ruler and pencil before the three layers were basted together.

NOTES ON QUILTING DESIGN FOR PIECED WORK AND APPLIQUÉ

I think it's important today that we give as much consideration to the quilting design as we give to the pieced or appliqué or other surface design of the quilt. The introduction of polyester battings has removed the necessity for close quilting; indeed, it has removed the necessity for any quilting at all. Since it's the quilting that defines the quilt, I think it must be given equal weight with any other pattern in the quilt surface.

Simply outlining or repeating the pieced or applied or other forms on the surface of the quilt is not always sufficient. The quilting design should, as much as possible, assume its own identity apart from those other forms. It must at the same time complement the rest of the activity in the surface.

The same push and pull that results from quilting some areas more closely than others in the whole-cloth quilt can be used effectively in other quilt surfaces. Dark colors can be pushed further back into the two-dimensional space of the quilt by quilting these closely. Unquilted light areas will move forward not only visually but also physically.

In *Fall's Island* (Figs. 7-12, 7-13, and 7-14 and Plate 1) Nancy Halpern has used a very fluid, freely drawn quilting design in combination with a crisply geometric pieced surface. The quilting design becomes a swirling mist around this vision of a pine-covered island. Although the forms in the pieced work bear no resemblance to the

Figure 7-12. *Fall's Island* by Nancy Halpern. 1979. 84 in. by 84 in. (213 cm by 213 cm). Cotton and cotton blends; polyester batting. Hand-pieced and hand-quilted.

Figure 7-13. Detail of *Fall's Island* by Nancy Halpern.

Figure 7-14. *Reversing Falls* by Nancy Halpern. This is the back of the quilt shown in Fig. 7-12.

forms created by the quilting, they are perfectly united in a correspondence suggested by their literal references.

What I find most impressive is that the quilting was actually designed and executed as a whole-cloth surface from the back of the quilt. *Reversing Falls* (Fig. 7-14) is the pure linear and low-relief image, a vortex of curvilinear forms swirling and blending and crossing with total abandon. The references to natural forms (including the figure of a seal swimming from the lower right toward the center) are as deliberate in the quilting as they are in the pieced work.

Beth Gutcheon takes a tongue-in-cheek look at a traditional pieced border design in *The Goose Is Loose* (Plate 28 and Fig. 7-15). I can't help chuckling to myself each time I see the liberation of these triangular forms from the geometric convention in which they have surrounded countless quilts. Despite the fact that they remain triangles after fleeing that regimentation, they take on, by association, a much more figurative quality.

Figure 7-15. *The Goose Is Loose* by Beth Gutcheon. Copyright 1979. 72 in. by 79 in. (183 cm by 201 cm). Machine-pieced, hand-appliquéd, and hand-quilted cotton and cotton blends; polyester batting. Private collection.

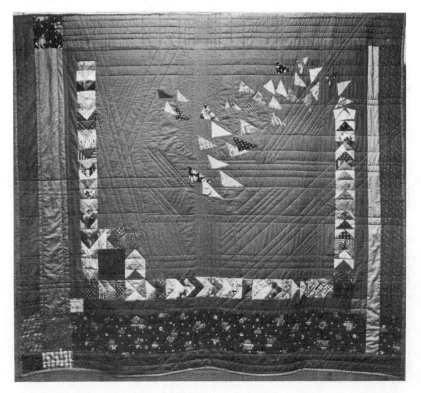

By contrast, the quilting design remains hard-edged, although it too flees from the inflexibility of the traditional filler pattern. The hand-stitched drawing defines transparent planes intersecting one another at various angles. Beth has effectively contrasted closely quilted with open areas in the large field of red. Her geese fly through an abstract linear network that recalls the spatial reconstructions of early twentieth-century Russian constructivist painters and sculptors.

In her series *Daylily, I* through *V* (Plates 23 through 27, and Fig. 7-16), Beth dissects the familiar North Carolina Lily pattern, eliminating a petal or two here and a stem there until the images become elusive remembrances of things past. As the disintegration of recognizable form proceeds, the shapes that remain become more entwined with the space that contains them. That space is again structured by hard-edged linear interrelationships that are united with the pieced image, yet exist apart from it. This is most obvious in *Daylily V* (Plate 27). This final piece in the series almost becomes whole-cloth.

Figure 7-16. *Daylily IV* by Beth Gutcheon. Copyright 1979. 23 in. by 25 in. (58.5 cm by 63.5 cm). Machine-pieced, hand-quilted cotton and cotton blends; polyester batting. Author's collection.

NEW EXPLORATIONS IN WHOLE-CLOTH

Wake-Up Quilt (Figs. 7-17 and 7-18), by Margaret Stephenson Coole, displays a surface image that is as bright and optimistic as the clearest sunrise. Large freehand-drawn curves divide the surface into bands containing ruled sets of parallel lines or more curved forms. Everything seems to be coming out of the upper left-hand corner of the quilt, and our eyes are continually redirected to that corner. Margaret creates rich visual textures and contrasts these effectively with the bold divisions that structure the surface.

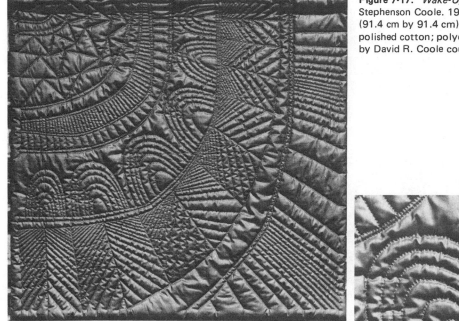

Figure 7-17. *Wake-Up Quilt* by Margaret Stephenson Coole. 1979. 36 in. by 36 in. (91.4 cm by 91.4 cm). Hand-quilted polished cotton; polyester batting. Photo by David R. Coole courtesy of the artist.

Figure 7-18. Detail of *Wake-Up Quilt* by Margaret Stephenson Coole.

In *Eccentric Circles* (Figs. 7-19 and 7-20) Maureen Barber defines groupings of large concentric circles with close background quilting. The smaller circles at the outside of the quilt catch light and seem almost stuffed against the more closely quilted background.

Virginia Anderson's quilt *Genesis* (Figs. 7-21 and 7-22) uses three repeat motifs in a grid format as shown in Fig. 7-11. At the center

Figure 7-19. *Eccentric Circles* by Maureen Barber. 1979. 36 in. by 36 in. (91.4 cm by 91.4 cm). Hand-quilted polished cotton; polyester batting. Photo by Karl Fox courtesy of the artist.

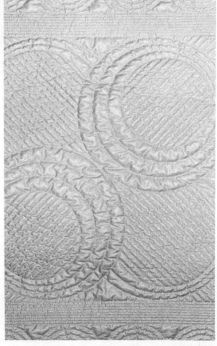

Figure 7-20. Detail of *Eccentric Circles* by Maureen Barber.

Figure 7-21. *Genesis* by Virginia Anderson. 1978. 36 in. by 36 in. (91.4 cm by 91.4 cm). Hand-quilted polished cotton; polyester batting.

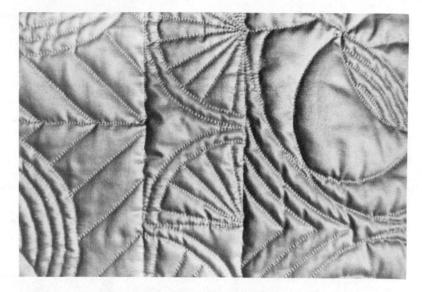

Figure 7-22. Detail of *Genesis* by Virginia Anderson.

she has arranged a random repeat with two overlapping circles, one open and one closely quilted. The parallel lines in the ground of these units join here and there with adjoining repeats. The inner border is a quarter-circle fan design, arranged at intervals to form semicircles and three-quarter circles. Another single repeat is used against itself in the outer border. Here Virginia turns the unit in every other interval so that the large forms connect to form soft S curves. The result is a complex surface of intense activity, executed with great skill.

Labyrinth (Figs. 7-23 and 7-24) by Maria McCormick-Snyder is as much a mathematical as an intellectual and artistic exercise. A latticework of positive and negative bands interweaves on the surface. Areas quilted in parallel lines ¼ in. (6 mm) apart clearly flatten out and raise the unquilted areas in higher relief. The mazelike pattern and the positive and negative reversals constantly challenge the eye to read the actual symmetry of the surface design.

Marie Kupferman used machine quilting to define the geometric pattern in the surface of *Thy Kingdom Come* (Figs. 7-25 and 7-26). Areas of close quilting contrast with larger open areas to highlight the central quatrefoil image.

In *Starting Point* Katie Pasquini uses radiation patterns to create a central medallion figure against a square-grid filler pattern (Fig. 7-27). The curves of the medallion are echoed by the curved extensions of the grid in the outer border.

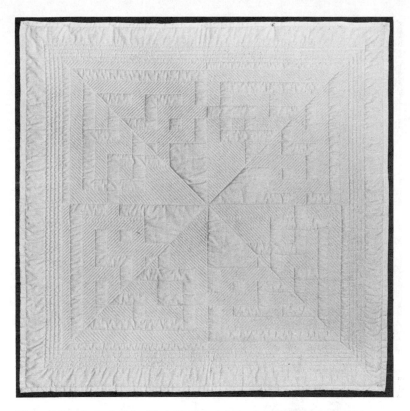

Figure 7-23. *Labyrinth* by Maria McCormick-Snyder. 1978. 44 in. by 44 in. (112 cm by 112 cm). Hand-quilted polished cotton; polyester batting. Photo courtesy of the artist.

Figure 7-24. Detail of *Labyrinth* by Maria McCormick-Snyder.

Figure 7-25. *Thy Kingdom Come* by Marie Kupferman. 1979. 42 in. by 42 in. (107 cm by 107 cm). Machine-quilted polished cotton; polyester batting.

Figure 7-26. Detail of *Thy Kingdom Come* by Marie Kupferman.

Figure 7-27. *Starting Point* by Katie Pasquini. 1979. 43 in. by 43 in. (109 cm by 109 cm). Hand-quilted polished cotton; polyester batting. Photo courtesy of the artist.

I used four linear repeats in *Suntreader/Monophony* (Figs. 7-28 and 7-29), twisting and turning them at random to arrive at the asymmetrical surface design. I first drew the horizontal and vertical lines on the fabric with ruler and pencil and I transferred the design with a perforated pattern and cinnamon as I did the quilting. After quilting the entire design, I cut the large circle from the square layers of material.

The title for this quilt came from a piece of music by that title written by the American composer Carl Ruggles, who in turn had drawn his inspiration from a poem by Robert Browning entitled "Pauline." The quilt is both a reflection on that piece of music and a reflection on the sun as mystical orb.

157

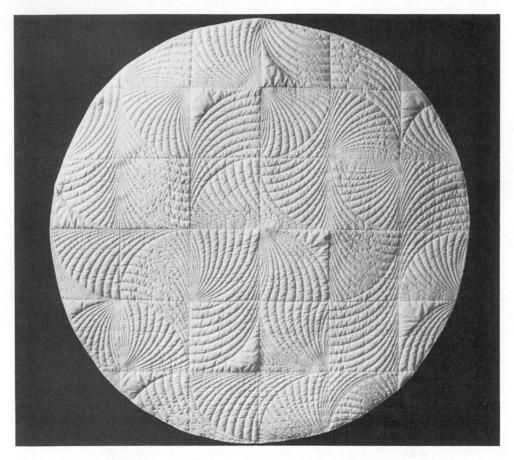

Figure 7-28. *Suntreader/Monophony* by the author. Copyright 1979. 60 in. (152 cm) diameter. Hand-quilted polished cotton; polyester batting.

Figure 7-29. Detail of *Suntreader/Monophony* by the author.

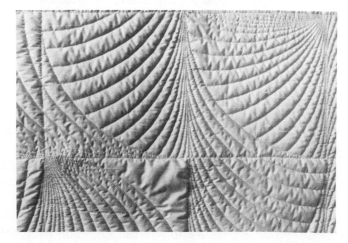

158

Elizabeth Gurrier's panels entitled *Double Angel Window* and *Single Deuce Window* (Figs. 7-30 and 7-31) push stuffed work to its limit as soft sculpture. In these pieces Elizabeth contrasts the smoothness of the tightly stuffed forms with the rough texture of cheesecloth. The fact that light can travel through the flat cheesecloth areas reinforces the idea that these panels are windows. In their form the panels also refer to the art and motifs of early New England gravestone carving. These figures, however, are not nearly as serious-minded, and in fact seem bemused by their otherworldliness.

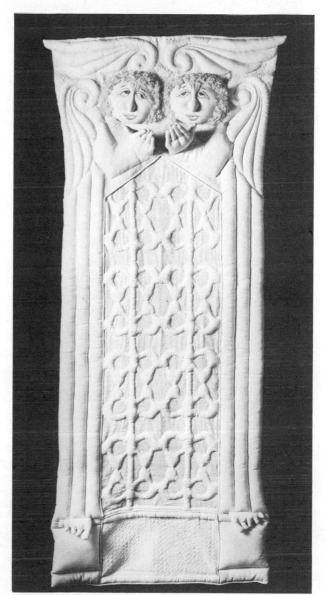

Figure 7-30. *Double Angel Window* by Elizabeth Gurrier. 1979. Unbleached muslin, cheesecloth, polyester batting and fill. Machine-quilted, embroidered, stuffed. Photo by Hamor courtesy of the artist.

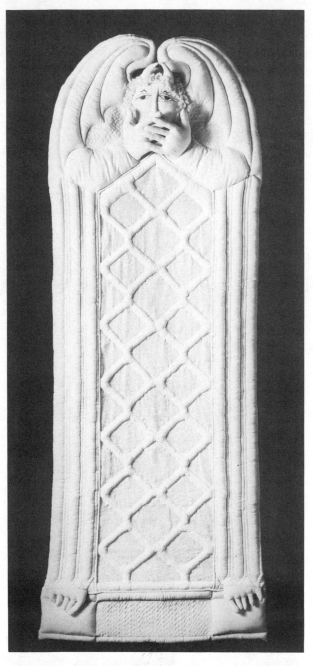

Figure 7-31. *Single Deuce Window* by Elizabeth Gurrier. 1979.
Unbleached muslin, cheesecloth, polyester batting and fill.
Machine-quilted, embroidered, stuffed. Photo by Hamor
courtesy of the artist.

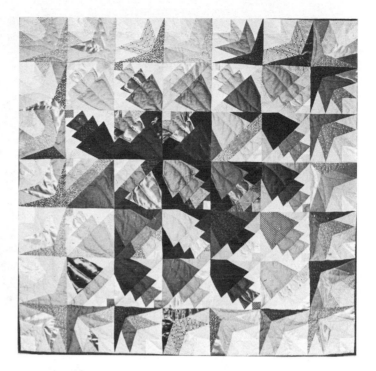

Appendix A

THE FLOWERING OF PIECED-QUILT DESIGN

During the 1920s and 1930s the quilt design studios of Ruby Short McKim popularized the geometric floral repeat pattern. Such blocks as Oriental Poppy, Trumpet Vine, Iris, and Pansy made the naturalistic representation of the appliqué quilt a possibility in pieced work as well.

The use of floral forms in pieced work remains an excellent color and design exercise. Flower blossoms are usually symmetrical forms. Some are bilateral in arrangement, but most embody radial symmetries of one kind or another. The leaf shapes that accompany those blossoms are also symmetrical figures, and often have equal value as repeat motifs in a pieced-quilt surface.

Complementary color contrasts are commonly displayed in floral forms, as are adjacent color contrasts. Violet, blue, and green combinations are just as frequently found as red and green or yellow and violet arrangements. Very subtle blendings of color in leaves and flower petals, however, reveal a full spectrum of hues that cannot fail to inspire the quilt artist.

Figure A-1. Detail, *Winter Cactus* by the author.

When considering a floral subject, whether in a photograph or from life, it's critical that you study the attitude and posture of the plant and its flower and capture that in the representation. A blossom that hangs suspended from a gracefully curved stem will lose its delicacy if depicted as a stiffened, erect figure. A flower that reaches out into space or encloses space will lose its character if made to occupy the entire repeat area as a flattened abstraction. It must be given two-dimensional space in which to move, much as it does as a real form in three-dimensional space.

At the same time plant forms must be simplified in the translation to geometric shapes in fabric. Look for the large shapes in the plant or flower and concentrate on these. Watch how contours of petals and leaves move and bend or curve. These postures will reveal the identifying profile of the plant.

You should also study the plant in regard to its color and how that color contrasts with colors around it. The color intensity of the blossom can be increased or decreased by changing the setting in which it's observed.

In *Winter Cactus* (Frontispiece, Fig. A-1, and Plate 32) I used the leaf and blossom arrangement of a Christmas cactus plant as the model for the pieced-block patterns. The leaf blocks at the center grow one from the end of another, as they do in the plant itself. The blossoms open into full flower in the outside border row of blocks.

Color for this quilt was based on the deep green and bright pink and red of the flowering plant itself. I selected all the green and red fabrics that I had on hand, including very light and very dark values. These were arranged in a surface that established a sense of space through the flickerings of light-reflective fabrics and the geometric fracturing of the surface.

In a similar way Nancy Halpern's *Rainy Day Crocuses* (Plate 29) reach out into space, but here the space is more literal. It is suggested by the unevenly dyed fabric that looks like a cloudy, misty sky. The blossoms here are vibrantly colored figures against the more subdued background. Not only does Nancy capture the physical attitude of the crocus, but she clearly depicts the flower as a herald of brightness and warmth.

Martha Maxfield's *Pansies* (Plate 30) occupy a surface space that is shallow by comparison with the space in the previous quilts. That space nevertheless reflects the image of the pansy blossom whose flattened face seems pressed against an imaginary two-dimensional plane. The bright spikes of yellow move from one flower to another, creating an allover repeat image that disguises the individual blossoms. Two repeat blocks were used here, alternated in diagonal rows.

Debra Hoss's *Cactus Quilt* (Plate 31) is a study based on a flowering cactus. The plant forms here dissolve into the mosaic of the pieced surface so that we are left with a brilliant color impression of the original figure. The repeat is an asymmetrical geometric composition that is arranged in quarter-turn. In that way the bright red blossoms open at the center of the quilt. The blue ground becomes a cool, open space that intensifies the colors in the plant forms.

Appendix B

NOTES ON FABRIC FOR QUILTS AND ITS CARE

Design problems such as that involving spontaneous color selections in Chapter 4 point out the advantages of having a varied selection of fabrics to work with. If you were to attempt to work out that particular exercise without repeating any fabrics, and you had sixteen blocks, each with eight shapes, or a total of 128 pieces, you would have to have at least that many compatible fabrics. This would suggest a large collection to draw from. Most of us would be hard pressed to put together a collection like that except over a long period of time.

If you are willing, however, to experiment with a wide variety of types of fabric, your resources may be far less limited. The traditional cottons can be used along with synthetic blends, satins, polished or glazed fabrics, metallics, corduroys, velveteens, velvets, and other fabrics. The experienced quiltmaker should have the confidence to adjust marking and sewing techniques to different materials and to employ them for different effects in the quilt surface.

Light holds fascination for the quiltmaker. Suggesting the movement of light across a surface, or creating the illusion of light coming out from the image, can be intriguing involvements. These effects can be aided by the use of both light-reflective and light-absorbent fabrics.

Satin-weave cottons and synthetics, polished cottons, and metallics and like fabrics reflect light, and so in actuality real light is introduced to the quilt surface. Satin-weave fabrics are especially active in this regard. Because of this weave, one piece of fabric, when cut and sewn at different angles and in different directions, will appear as a multiplicity of values of that color. When you move in front of pieced satins your perception of light reflections is changed. Even as natural or artificial light changes, so too does the quilt surface that contains satin-weave fabrics.

Cotton broadcloths, corduroys, velveteens, and velvets are light-absorbent fabrics. They present their color with far less variability than light-reflective fabrics. However, corduroys change their appearance when the direction of the nap is varied, as do velvets and velveteens to an even greater degree. These fabrics have the additional tactile appeal that comes with their more highly textured surfaces.

Although working with a large variety of fabric types might put the sewing skills of a beginner to a real test, the experienced quiltmaker should be able to adapt sewing techniques to these materials. For fabrics such as corduroy and velveteen, hand-piecing stitches will necessarily be a bit larger. Some satin-weave acetates will resist the hand-guided needle, so fewer stitches can be taken at one time. Satin-weave cottons (sateens) are generally softer and will require finer stitches. Quilting stitches on velveteen or velvet will disappear into the nap of the fabric if they are too small, so an expert quilter will deliberately increase the stitch size when working on these surfaces.

When practical, machine piecing can be your answer to the use of a range of different fabrics. Heavier fabrics such as corduroy and velveteen are more easily sewn by machine. Many drapery and upholstery fabrics, appealing because of their wide range of textures, are too heavy to be easily sewn by hand and require machine construction.

How you intend to use a quilt will also have a bearing on the types of fabrics you use. A wall quilt that gets no wear and needs little or no cleaning can employ a wider range of fabrics in its surface than a functional bed quilt. The bed quilt that is handled daily, folded and unfolded, sat upon and slept under will need cleaning several times a year, and perhaps more frequently. It should be made of fabrics that can withstand such use and the wear of occasional cleanings, whether by water wash or by dry treatments.

Delicate fabrics, such as satin acetate, cotton sateen, silk, and taffeta, wear well in the wall quilt that receives little handling. However, you should be aware that light, both natural and artificial, can affect these fabrics even more noticeably and more quickly than it affects cotton and cotton-blend broadcloths. Display lighting of any quilt should be kept as far away from the surface as possible. Indirect spotlighting reflected onto the quilt from a white ceiling or wall surface is preferable to direct spotlighting. When the texture of the quilting design needs to be emphasized, you can direct a small spot at the quilt from a side angle to complement the general reflected lighting. This reduces the high risk of fading that comes with rows of intense spots hung too close to the quilt surface. Direct sunlight should never be allowed to shine on any quilt.

A wall quilt, like any other stationary interior object, will gather dust over a period of time. It should be removed regularly, at least three or four times a year. Small quilts can be shaken gently at more frequent intervals.

The best method for removing dust from a quilt surface is by vacuuming. The quilt surface is protected with a square yard of fiberglass screening, available in most home maintenance centers. Lay the quilt on a flat surface and cover a section with the screening. Use a small hand-held vacuum if you have one, gently passing it over the screen to loosen dust on the quilt surface. A brushless attachment is preferred. You can use a regular domestic vacuum cleaner providing the suction is not strong enough to lift the screening or the quilt. The screening prevents scratching or marking of the quilt surface.

Appendix C

NOTES ON TAKING YOUR QUILT'S PICTURE

When I finish a new quilt, the first thing I do is photograph it. I've usually put so much time and effort into making the piece that I want to be sure to have photographic reproductions of it just in case (heaven forbid!) something should happen to it.

I know also that I'll need to have color slides of the quilt to submit to exhibition juries, to show in lectures and workshops, to send to galleries or others inquiring about the availability of work for sale or display, and to share or exchange with associates.

I've always photographed my own work, for a number of reasons. First, I enjoy doing it. Photography interests me, and my stubborn and stumbling search for the perfect representation of each new quilt provides a constant challenge. My experiences behind the camera have been almost entirely unscientific, but I know I have a rapport with my subject that no professional photographer would be able to feel. When I photograph a quilt, I know exactly how much I want to emphasize the quilting design on the surface, and how much or how little light I want to see on reflective fabrics.

A second reason has been economic. Professional photography is expensive. For the cost of one original slide from a studio, I can buy two or three rolls of 36-exposure film. For the cost of 10 duplicates of that one original slide I can have 72 of my own originals commercially processed. (Clearly, the cost of a 35-mm camera, a lens, and a few lights represents no small investment. If you don't own a camera and feel that you don't want to be bothered learning how to use one to photograph quilts, then the professional craft photographer is a good alternative.)

Finally, I find I'm frequently in the position of completing a new quilt on the day it must be sent off or delivered to an exhibition. Before it goes, I must have slides of it, and there's usually no time to rush it off to have someone else photograph it.

Perhaps you've made the same choice for similar reasons. If so, you want the most accurate representation you can get. When you send a slide off to an exhibition jury, you want the color to be as close as possible to that of the actual object. You want the film neither over- nor underexposed. You want the picture sharply focused, and you want the object to fill as much of the frame as possible. Finally, you want nothing in the slide that will draw attention from or interfere with the quilt.

THE CAMERA AND ACCESSORIES

Since I'm basing these comments on my own trial-and-error experiences, I'll be referring only to the use of a 35-mm single-lens reflex camera. Today, most quiltmakers who regularly photograph their own work use this type of camera.

I assume that you know how your camera operates. You should know how to select the proper exposure for a given shutter speed by reading the built-in light meter if your camera has one, or a hand-held exposure meter if not. Perhaps you own one of the newer cameras that automatically sets the shutter speed when you select the aperture setting on the lens.

The standard 50- to 55-mm lenses that come with most camera outfits are suitable for taking good slides of most of your work. For details, they will allow you to focus as close as 1½ feet (0.45 m). If you are photographing large quilts, however, you will need a greater distance between the camera and the quilt surface in order to get the entire quilt in the frame. For example, if the quilt measures 90 in. by 90 in. (229 cm by 229 cm), you will need to hold the camera about 6 yards (5.5 m) from the object. For many of us, this precludes indoor photography for lack of space. This also becomes a problem when photographing quilt exhibits. Large pieces cannot be shot in their entirety unless there is enough room to step back far enough.

The answer to this problem is the 28-mm wide-angle lens. With this lens that same 90-in.- (229-cm)-square quilt could be photographed full-frame at about 9.5 feet, that is, at about 3 yards (2.7 m) or half the distance needed with a standard lens. In a shallow room this could mean the difference between shooting the quilt, in whole or in part, or waiting for agreeable weather and outdoor light conditions. The wide-angle lens works well for details also, and will allow you to focus as close as 1 foot (30.5 cm) from your subject.

An indispensable tool for taking sharply focused slides of your quilts is a tripod. You simply cannot rely on your ability to hold the camera steady enough when you are shooting a flat object that may be made up of hundreds of tiny printed fabric shapes. Nor can you expect the quilting lines to be well defined if there's any movement of the camera.

The tripod doesn't have to be fancy or expensive. Its purpose is to provide a solid, stationary support, and that's all it need do. You should be able to adjust it so that you can raise the camera 60 in. to 72 in. (152 cm to 183 cm) from the floor. At about this height, you will be able to align the lens with the approximate center of the quilt under average hanging conditions. A lightweight tripod that folds compactly is useful also for photographing work in exhibits.

When shooting your own work indoors, you will need to provide lighting suitable for the type of film you're using. To do this, you will need two or more floodlight reflectors. These can be purchased inexpensively with squeeze-type clamp-on fittings, but this type necessitates having something to clamp the reflectors to. Choosing reflectors with telescoping tripod stands solves this problem.

A flash unit can also be used. Head-on flash lighting of the quilt surface, however, washes out the subtle shadows cast by the indentations of the quilting lines. With large quilts, direct flash lighting tends to illuminate the center of the quilt, while the outside edges are underexposed.

BACKDROPS

One concern many quiltmakers share in regard to photographing their quilts is the backdrop. Under ideal circumstances, we take advantage of a large white wall. This shows the quilt with nothing in the background to distract.

If you have a workroom with a fairly large wall, this can be painted white and used as a backdrop.

If no plain wall is available, there are alternatives. The quilt can be photographed on any large, flat surface whether it be a wallpapered wall, the side of a cement block garage, a chain link fence, or a weathered board barn. Later, the processed image of the quilt can be isolated with slide masking tape (as demonstrated).

The quilt can also be isolated from the distraction of any of these surfaces by placing white paper around its perimeter. The paper may be in sheet or roll form, and is tacked or taped to the wall surface. The quilt is then positioned over this, so that at least several inches of paper are exposed all around, as in Fig. C-1. Later, the images will be masked so that only a narrow white space is exposed beyond the edges of the quilt (see Fig. C-2).

Very light-colored quilts as well as all-white whole-cloth quilts are better photographed against a dark surface. Photographer's seamless backdrop papers come in a range of widths and colors and are suitable for covering interior walls. They are available at most large photo supply centers. The quilts in Figs. 7-28 and 4-50 were photographed against seamless black paper hung against a white wall. Small

Figure C-1. Pieced work being photographed on the side of a building. The white paper isolates the object from the wall.

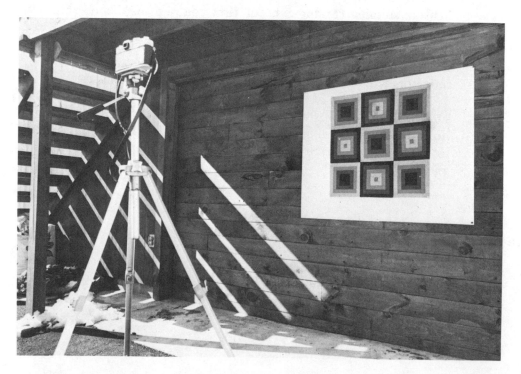

Figure C-2. What the camera sees. The wood exposed around the paper can be masked off. The camera could have been moved closer to the subject to eliminate that exposed wood from the picture frame.

sheets of black paper can be used as inserts around the perimeter of a light-colored quilt as described above with white paper. The quilt in Fig. 7-1 was photographed this way.

If you are serious about your work and expect it to be taken seriously by others, you should present it as professionally as possible. Hanging a quilt from a clothesline isn't even recommended after washing, and is certainly no way to present work for review. Draping your quilt over an antique settee may be decorative and nostalgically appealing, but will say less about your quilt than about your own romantic yearnings for times past.

LIGHTING AND FILM

These two areas of quilt photography are inseparable. They also present the biggest problems to quiltmakers doubling as amateur photographers.

One thing that I consider important enough to emphasize is that you will probably need to experiment with various films and with various forms of lighting before finding the combination that does the most justice to your work. One thing that can never be conveyed in a slide of a quilt is the tactile appeal that the object has on the viewer standing in front of the real thing. Short of that, however, you should be able to give a good representation of the two-dimensional design, the colors, the quilting design (if any), and how well the piece is made.

Kodachrome films provide excellent color rendition with different light sources and are a practical choice. Kodachrome 25 (ASA 25) provides excellent color saturation and its slow speed results in very fine grain. Kodachrome 64 (ASA 64) is faster, but at the sacrifice of some of the color intensity and grain. If you compared two slides of the same quilt, taken under the same lighting conditions but one with ASA 25 film and the other with ASA 64 film, you'd probably notice little difference. The differences would appear, however, if the two slides were projected side by side onto a screen from across an auditorium.

Both these films are balanced for use in daylight or with electronic flash or blue flashbulbs.

If you are photographing out-of-doors, use Kodachrome 25. When time allows, wait for a day that is lightly overcast, yet bright. Strong sunlight will change photographic conditions quickly, affecting even reflected light on the surface of your quilt. It will also tend to give additional warmth to the color tone. Both the quilt and the camera should be in light shade, with no direct sunlight shining on the quilt or into the camera lens. Direct sunlight on the quilt surface washes out color and will accentuate the quilting too harshly. It will also emphasize any irregularity in the smoothness of the surface.

I feel that outdoor quilt photography is ultimately unsuitable. Lighting is too difficult to control, and virtually impossible to duplicate when you do get good results. Too often you must wait days or longer for the right conditions. When you're waiting for the snow to melt, or the rain to stop, or the sun to come out or go in, or the wind to die down, you sense a lack of freedom that makes studio photography very appealing.

You can photograph your quilts indoors with a minimum of equipment. If most of your work is smaller than about 48 in. by 48 in. (122 cm by 122 cm) you can get away with two floodlights positioned at side angles to the surface of the quilt. An indoor equivalent of Kodachrome 25 film is Kodachrome 40 Type A (ASA 40). This film is balanced for use with 3400K Photoflood bulbs. Two bulbs, 500 watts each, will be sufficient for smaller works. For larger quilts, use at least four bulbs in floodlight reflectors. (These reflectors make excellent supplementary lighting fixtures around the quiltmaker's work space. Substitute regular incandescent bulbs for the floodlights when the latter are not needed.)

You will need to experiment with the positions of the floodlights until you see that your quilt is evenly illuminated (see Fig. C-3). If your quilt contains reflective fabrics, you may encounter glare or extreme highlights that will be distracting in the final image. Try bouncing light off the ceiling to soften these highlights. One or two floods are directed at the ceiling or at white walls perpendicular to the quilt. Large sheets of white paper may also be used for this pur-

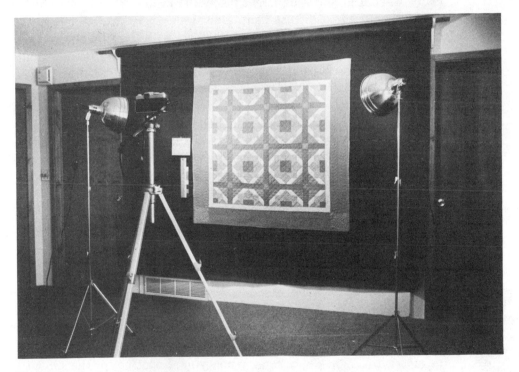

Figure C-3. Studio setup with black paper backdrop.

pose. The other floods are directed at the quilt to emphasize any quilting on the surface. Such indirect light will also help to flatten the appearance of a quilt that is not hanging quite flush with the wall.

(Here an ethical question arises. Is it fair to use photographic techniques to disguise imperfections in the quilt itself? When the photographic reproduction is being submitted in competition, and selection of the actual work is based on the slide or print, I submit that it isn't fair to the artist, to the jurors, or to the other competitors.)

Both Kodachrome 25 and Kodachrome 64 can be used with an

electronic flash unit. If you prefer the flash, or if you are shooting at a show or exhibit where use of photofloods is impractical, bounce the light off a ceiling or adjoining white wall or off a white card that you position at an angle to the quilt. When doing this, you may want to take several shots at different exposures to get one that is correct.

I have had good results using Kodak Ektachrome 160 Professional (ASA 160) film with 500-watt, 3200K tungsten flood lamps. I set four reflectors six to eight feet from the quilt and at angles to it. Occasionally one or perhaps two lamps are aimed at the ceiling, especially when I'm shooting larger pieces. Translucent reflector shields can also be used to diffuse light. During daylight hours I darken the room so that natural light will not interfere with the film color.

If time allows, I like to shoot one experimental roll of a new quilt, changing the positions and the directions of the flood lamps, as well as the exposure settings on the lens. Next to the quilt I attach a sheet of paper on which I record the shutter speed and exposure, as well as the type of film, the number of lights, and how many lamps, if any, were used to provide indirect reflected light. This provides me with a permanent record for each frame on the roll. When more slides are needed at a later date, the conditions that provided the best-quality image can be more accurately duplicated.

This film also works well in museum or gallery settings, where tungsten spotlights are frequently used to illuminate quilt displays.

Figure C-4. Quilt as photographed against backdrop, with data card and color patch card.

Flash photography is often prohibited in these settings. In this case, tungsten 160 is a good alternative.

If you photograph work for color reproduction in a magazine, catalog, or book, you may want to include in the photograph a Kodak color control patch card (see Fig. C-4). This is a printed photographic color scale that allows the printer to compare the color of the subject (the quilt) with standard printing colors. Color variations in the photographic image can be adjusted to achieve more accuracy in the final reproduction.

MASKING TRANSPARENCIES

When a slide of a quilt or any flat artwork is projected, large fields of empty white space around the quilt are unnecessary, and trees or garage doors or sagging fabric backdrops are distracting.

The image of the quilt can be isolated by using silver slide masking tape available in photo supply centers. This tape is very thin and its surface reflects heat from the projection lamp, thus reducing the possibility that the slide will warp. Black vinyl electrical tape is not recommended because it absorbs heat and will shrink and pull back over a period of time, leaving an adhesive residue as a border around the projected image.

Two types of slide mount are commonly used. Cardboard mounts are heat-sealed, while plastic mounts snap together. These are easier to work with than cardboard mounts because you don't risk warping the slide as you do when sealing with a hot iron. Their disadvantage lies in the possibility that the transparency will loosen in the mount and shift out of position.

To remove a transparency from a cardboard mount, cut across the mount with a razor-bladed knife about halfway between the top of the transparency opening and the top of the mount. Fold back the cardboard at this line as in Fig. C-5 and slide out the transparency. To remove a transparency from a plastic mount, simply pull the top and back halves apart.

There are dispensers available for cutting the masking tape. I simply place the roll in a cellophane tape dispenser, cutting short lengths as I need them. When masking off a quilt image, I prefer leaving a narrow space around the edge of the quilt rather than taping right up to the edge. The tape is applied to the glossy, front side of the transparency (Fig. C-6). This is the side that will face the projection lamp. The duller, emulsion side faces the screen. Be careful to

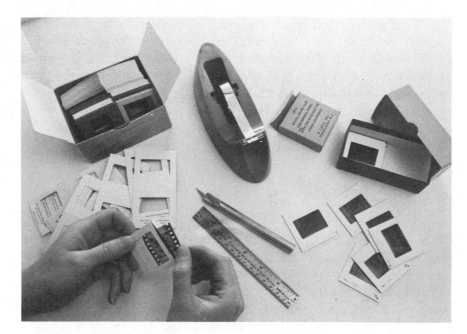

Figure C-5. Removing slide from mount.

Figure C-6. Applying silver masking tape to glossy face of slide.

avoid leaving fingerprints and other marks on the surfaces of the transparency.

When the tape is in place, slide the transparency into the mount. Cardboard mounts must be heat-sealed. Use an iron set at a wool setting, or just slightly cooler. Carefully touch the iron to the mount for a few seconds. If the iron is too hot or applied for too long a period, it can easily warp the transparency.

Even the best slide cannot fully portray the beauty of a finely designed and crafted quilt. It should, however, give a good impression of this beauty, leaving no doubt in the mind of the viewer (see Fig. C-7).

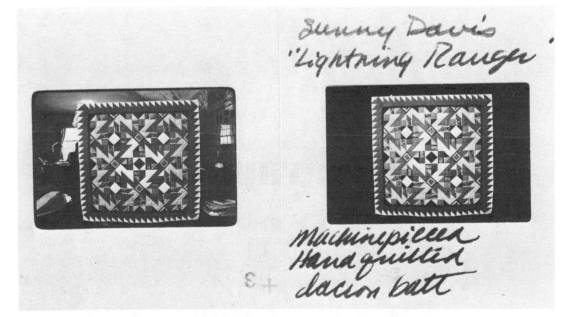

Figure C-7. Two slides of the same quilt. The slide on the right is masked to the edges of the quilt. It was photographed exactly as was the slide on the left, in which a room interior is visible. The quilt was being held up by two volunteers.

Bibliography

The following works are those that I find myself referring to regularly or that have inspired me in my teaching or in my own work.

QUILT HOW-TO

Gutcheon, Beth, *The Perfect Patchwork Primer*. Baltimore: Penguin Books, 1974. Beth's delivery is fresh and energetic, her counsel wise, and the drawings of dozens of block patterns are well executed and complete.

James, Michael, *The Quiltmaker's Handbook*. Englewood Cliffs, N.J.: Prentice-Hall, Inc., 1978. Perhaps I can't be really objective about this one, but I feel it contains a thorough, well-illustrated treatment of traditional quiltmaking techniques and enough contemporary quilt work to keep your mind buzzing for weeks. It's the book I wish I'd had when I first started making quilts.

Beyer, Jinny, *Patchwork Patterns*. McLean, Virginia: EPM Publications, 1979. Although I don't use folded-paper pattern drafting, I enjoy studying the drawings in this helpful guide to symmetrical pieced design.

TWO-DIMENSIONAL DESIGN PRINCIPLES

Bothwell, Dorr, and Marlys Frey, *Notan: The Dark-Light Principle of Design*. New York: Van Nostrand Reinhold Company, 1968. Every concept presented in this book is indispensable to a clear understanding of two- and three-dimensional design.

Dondis, Donis A., *A Primer of Visual Literacy*. Cambridge, Mass.: The MIT Press, 1973. The elements of visual design are given a sensitive and detailed treatment in this volume. I think that quilt design instructors will find this book invaluable as a resource on the elements of design.

Proctor, Richard M., *The Principles of Pattern*. New York: Van Nostrand Reinhold Company, 1969. A collection of visually stimulating pattern images that you'll enjoy wandering through when in a contemplative mood.

Wong, Wucius, *Principles of Two-Dimensional Design*. New York: Van Nostrand Reinhold Company, 1972. This is one of the most clearly illustrated and succinct guides to two-dimensional design in print.

COLOR

Albers, Josef, *Interaction of Color*. New Haven: Yale University Press, 1971.

Itten, Johannes, *The Art of Color*. New York: Van Nostrand Reinhold Company, 1973.

Both these books force you to look at color analytically and critically. They are based on their authors' painstakingly developed color courses, and for the initiate they are better understood as accompaniments to a color course or as refreshers afterward.

Needleman, Carla, *The Work of Craft*. New York: Alfred A. Knopf, Inc., 1979. Read this book in small doses, and take the time to think about what the author says.

Pye, David, *The Nature and Aesthetics of Design*. New York: Van Nostrand Reinhold Company, 1979. A scholarly and penetrating study of design as art and art as design, this book speaks eloquently of the relationship of design to life and living.

Pye, David, *The Nature and Art of Workmanship*. New York: Van Nostrand Reinhold Company, 1971. The author speaks of craftsmanship and what it means to be a craftsman, and of the place of the crafts in contemporary society.

Index

Amish, 37
Anderson, Virginia:
  Genesis, 152 (Figs. 7-21, 7-22)
  Whirligig, 33, Plate 2
Art:
  decorative, 3
  definitions, 3
  fine art, 3
  folk or naive art, 3
Asymmetrical blocks:
  multiple repeat, 13, 14 (Figs. 2-11,
    2-12), 22
Asymmetry, 12
  in curved seam patterns, 60
Axes, corner-to-corner:
  examples, 9 (Fig. 2-5)

Balance:
  asymmetrical, 12
  symmetrical, 9, 12
Barber, Maureen:
  Eccentric Circles, 152 (Figs. 7-19,
    7-20)

Barnes, Françoise:
  Black Metamorphosis, 103 (Figs.
    5-14, 5-15)
  Blue Metamorphosis, 101 (Fig.
    5-13), Plate 19
  Escape, 103 (Fig. 5-16)
  Eyes of Isis, 103 (Figs. 5-17, 5-18)
Barn Raising (Log Cabin), 111
Batting, 138
  in Log Cabin quilts, 124
  polyester fleece batting, 124
Bias, 74
Borders:
  pieced, 25
  rationale for, 26
  sources of, 26
Burke, Janie:
  Curved Seam Study, 64 (Figs. 4-14,
    4-15)
  Farmscape Times Three, 33, Plate 6
  Fruit Slices, 83 (Figs. 4-46,
    4-47)
  Rainbow Sherbets, 82, Plate 5

Cogswell, Nell:
  Aquarius Quilt, 36, 37, Plate 3
Color:
  adjacent, 46
  complementary, 45, 161
  cool, 48
  density, 37
  opacity, 37
  pure color, 36, 39
    effect of white on, 37
  temperature, 36, 45, 47
  tertiary, 38
  warm, 48
Color interactions:
  additive, 46
  subtractive, 47, 120
Color wheel, 36, 39, 44, Plate 33
Coole, Margaret Stephenson:
  Wake-Up Quilt, 151 (Figs. 7-17,
    7-18)
Courthouse Steps, 116
Crow, Nancy:
  February Study 2, 52, 83, 100,
    Plate 20
  March Study, 52, 83, 100, Plate 22
  Matisse Plain, 52, 100, Plate 16
  Newe II, 100, Plate 21
Curved seam, 54-86
  characteristics of, 54, 61, 62
  exercises, 57-62
  hand-piecing, 76-79
  machine-piecing, 79-82
  pressing, 78, 81
  repeat patterns, 59-62
  traditional patterns, 54 (Fig. 4-1)
Curves:
  clipping, 74
  concave, 74
  drafting of, 65
  tapered, 70-73
    pressing of, 81

Davis, Sunny:
  Lightning Ranger, 29, 31 (Fig.
    2-28), Plate 7
    discussion of border in, 26
Donnell-Vogt, Radka:
  Wholeness, 104, Plate 18

English paper patchwork, 82

Fabric:
  choosing for quilts, 164
  effect of light on, 166
  grain, 74
    importance of in strip piecing,
      89

polished cotton, 138
Filler patterns for quilting, 140

Geometric design, 7
Gurrier, Elizabeth:
  Double Angel Window, 159 (Fig.
    7-30)
  Single Deuce Window, 159 (Fig.
    7-31)
Gutcheon, Beth:
  Day Lily Series I-V, 150 (Fig.
    7-16), Plates 23-27
  The Goose Is Loose, 52, 149, 150
    (Fig. 7-15), Plate 28

Halpern, Nancy:
  Fall's Island, 36, 147 (Figs. 7-12,
    7-13, 7-14), Plate 1
  Flying Carpet, 10, 11 (Figs. 2-7,
    2-8)
  Rainy Day Crocuses, 163, Plate 29
  Reversing Falls, 149 (Fig. 7-14)
Hoss, Debra:
  Cactus Quilt, 163, Plate 31

Intensity, 36
  definition, 45
  relativity of, 119, 162
Intensity change, 119

James, Michael:
  Aurora, 51, 53, 83, 85 (Figs. 4-48,
    4-49), Plates 10, 11
  Dawn Nebula, 53, 85, Plate 9
  Ivy Covered Wall, 50, Plate 12
  Moonshadow, 51, 86, Plate 15
  Poppies, 129 (Figs. 6-34, 6-35),
    Plate 13
  Suntreader/Monophony, 146, 157
    (Figs. 7-28, 7-29)
  Suntreader/Polyphony, 86 (Figs.
    4-50, 4-51), Plate 14
  Winter Cactus, Frontispiece, 162
    (Fig. A-1), Plate 32

Kupferman, Marie:
  Thy Kingdom Come, 154 (Figs.
    7-25, 7-26)

Light and dark contrast, 35, 36
  in asymmetrical pattern, 12
  in curved seam patterns, 62
  in Log Cabin, 111, 114
  in opposite-sequence block, 118
  in repeat pattern, 27 (Fig. 2-12)
  in strip piecing, 95, 98

Line:
  as element in curved seam, 56
  in the whole-cloth quilt, 139
Log Cabin Variation, 131 (Figs. 6-36, 6-37), Plate 17
  center shape variations, 109, 110
  corner-square block, 108 (Fig. 6-5)
  Courthouse Steps, 110, 111
  diagonal light/dark structure, 107
  machine techniques, 121-28
  off-center block, 109 (Fig. 6-4)
  Pineapple, 38, 111 (Fig. 6-10), Plate 36
  pyramid illusion, 48, 49 (Fig. 3-9)
  size gradations, 108, 110 (Fig. 6-3)
  value change in, 42

McCormick-Snyder, Maria:
  Art Deco, 133 (Figs. 6-38, 6-39)
  Labyrinth, 154 (Figs. 7-23, 7-24)
  Log Cabin Variation, 131 (Figs. 6-36, 6-37), Plate 17
  quilting of, 141
  Off-Center Log Cabin Sampler, 116, 120 (Fig. 6-17)
Machine piecing:
  curved seam, 73-82
  Log Cabin, 121-28
  strip pieced work, 90
McKim, Ruby Short, 161
Maxfield, Martha:
  Leaves, 63 (Fig. 4-13)
  Pansies, 163, Plate 30
Monochromatic value gradation, 43, 44, 98, 119

Off-center Log Cabin block, 109, 120 (Fig. 6-4)
Overlap:
  in spatial illusions, 48

Pasquini, Katie:
  Starting Point, 154 (Fig. 7-27)
Perforated patterns:
  for quilting design transfer, 146
Photographing quilts, 167-77
Pieced work:
  floral themes in, 161
Pile fabrics:
  cutting, 75
Pineapple Log Cabin, 118 (Fig. 6-21), Plate 36
Polychromatic value gradation, 44, 49, 98, 120
  scale, Plate 33

Pressed piecing, 106, 121
Primary colors, 37, 44

Quilt:
  as art object, 5
  care of, 165, 166
Quilting, 136-60
  contrast in, 143
  fabrics suitable for, 138
  filler patterns, 140
  hand, 137
  machine, 138
  marking design on fabric, 146
  stuffed, 143
  surface texture, 136
The Quiltmaker's Handbook, 146
Quiltmaking:
  as art form, 4
  as decorative art, 4, 5
  as fine art, 5
  as folk art, 5
  in Middle East, 2
  social aspects of, 2
  traditional attitudes toward, 5

Radial symmetry, 9
Radiation patterns, 141
Repeat block surface, 7

Sateen, 165
Satin, 138, 165
  cutting, 75
  pressing, 78
Seam gauge:
  improvised, 80
  on machine, 80
Seminole patchwork, 87
Sewing machine:
  care, 87, 88
Simultaneous contrast, 47
Size gradation:
  Log Cabin, 115
  strip piecing, 96
Smith, Be
  Storm Over Alexandria, 134 (Fig. 6-41)
  Tennessee Sunrise, 133 (Fig. 6-40)
Space, 43
  in curved seam patterns, 62
  two-dimensional, 48
Spaeth, Peggy:
  Boxes and Stars, 38, Plate 8
Spatial illusions:
  function of overlap in, 48
  function of proportion in, 48
  in strip piecing, 95

symmetrical distributions of, 9 (Fig. 2-4)

Straight Furrow (Log Cabin), 111
Stripe fabrics:
 in strip piecing, 97, 98
Strip piecing, 87-105
 design, 95
 marking fabric for, 88
 seam allowance, 89
 sewing, 90
 size gradation in, 96
Stuffed quilting, 143
Surface design, 5
Symmetrical blocks:
 multiple repeat, 10
Symmetry, 7, 8
 axial, 8
 bilateral, 8
  in pieced floral patterns, 161
 quadrilateral, 8
 radial, 9
  in pieced floral patterns, 161

Temperature:
 in color, 47
Temperature contrast, 120
 in curved seam, 62
 in strip piecing, 96, 98
Templates:
 for hand-pieced curves, 67
 for machine-pieced curves, 73
 materials for, 67

Texture:
 in whole-cloth quilts, 142
Translucence, 37
Transparency, 50

Value:
 in complementary harmonies, 46
 definition, 39
 pure, 39
 relativity, 119
Value change, 41, 42, 119
Value gradation, 36, 41
 in curved seam patterns, 62
 in Log Cabin, 115
 monochromatic, 43, 44
 polychromatic, 44
 in strip piecing, 95
Value scale, 40, 41, Plate 33
Van Buskirk, Joy, 28, 30 (Fig. 2-27)
Velveteen, 138, 165
 cutting, 75
 pressing, 78

Warm colors, 48
Whole-cloth quilt, 137
 design, 139
 texture, 142